Not Abandoned

To Uncle Dan,

"I know what I'm doing. I have it all planned out — plans to take care of you, not abandon you. Plans to give you the future you hope for." Jeremiah 29:11, The Message

Not abandoned,
Dianne Porter

Not Abandoned

Dianne Esau Porter

ISBN-13: 9781514322901
ISBN-10: 1514322900

Cover photo by Ariel Oliver Photography (ariel@arieloliver.com) at Rampart Range Reservoir in Woodland Park, Colorado

Dedication

This story of God's faithfulness is dedicated to my children Vonda, Sean and Nicole and my grandchildren Timothy, Samuel, Elijah, Ezra, Addison and Declan.

Special thanks to my husband Rick and daughter Vonda who helped with editing and daughter Nicole who assisted with the cover. Thanks also to several publishers who affirmed to me that my story is worth publishing.

Table of Contents

Foreword

THERE'S AN OLD gospel song. You can probably find some grainy, scratchy version on YouTube. It concludes this way, "I will tell the saints and angels as I lay my burden down, Jesus led me all the way."

We can theologize about the content. There's more than a hint of "woe is me" spirituality in there. Why on earth did you ever pick that burden up? Jesus invited us to Himself because, among other things, "His burden is light." He also warned us about those who "tie up heavy burdens, hard to bear, and lay them on people's shoulders." Nevertheless, there are times in our lives where the burdens get ahead of our ability to hand them off. But even then, "He giveth more grace when the burdens grow greater." Heavy loads are opportunities (if you haven't figured it out, the category is "Old Gospel Songs" for $200, Alex) for "every burden becomes a blessing, when I know my Lord is nigh."

Dianne Esau Porter wants to "tell the saints and angels" a story. It's a story of burdens and blessings. But unlike the song implies, she wants to tell it now. She wants to tell you, saint, and if any angels are eavesdropping, good on 'em! After all, the Holy Spirit through Peter revealed that even angels "long to look" into the relationship of Jesus with the redeemed!

There will be some great story-telling in the age to come. Imagine when you bump into the Apostle Paul and he says, "So, tell me about *your* Damascus Road." Or, Mary the Mother of Jesus wants you to share how the deepest losses of life were redeemed in God's greater purposes. Presumably by the time she asks, you will know even if you're in the dark just now. "Hey Noah, how'd that whole two-by-two thing work?" And perhaps

Christ Himself will turn to beloved Dianne Esau Porter and say, "I did not get a chance to read your book while I was making intercession for you from the right hand of the Father but I was leading you all the way. Tell me about it. Take your time. I want to hear it through your tender heart and passionate, artistic sense for the deepest of feelings."

Long hours of reflection on the last few painful, wonderful decades of our lives have produced a story worth telling and reading filled with the accumulated advice of many counselors, not the least of which is Dianne herself. She is a saver. And for your good she has saved the content of her/our journey and the supportive persons past and present who have carried her. Reading. Journaling. Singing. Listening. Praying. Healing. She has to tell you what she has learned and how it cultivated her growth as a beloved daughter of God.

In her own sweet way, she's told it without tossing anyone under the bus. She could have named names. But as much as possible she's worked at forgiving those who wounded, some knowingly, others oblivious. Some acted out of ill intent and others, indeed most, were wielded as chisels in the sculpture of her life and ours by the Benevolent Controller of All Things. She was shaped in the process. She prays that no chisels were harmed in the making of this story. Her hard effort at forgiveness has been a model for me and sometimes a rebuke, for I've surely fallen short of her grace.

I often go around saying that "the world doesn't need another book." I'm wrong. That's just my faux excuse for never getting around to writing my own. The truth is the world needs everyone's book. The saints and angels need to be told sooner rather than later. The world especially needs to hear from those who have traversed the valley of the shadow and lived to tell about it. Moreover we need to practice our stories on one another. Jesus might ask someday.

Thanks, Di, for telling your story to others and to me. You know I'm no angel. But by God's grace I am a saint. And if I am, how much more are you?

Rick Porter

Preface

Everybody can whine about their job. There are ups and downs. But it's easy to conclude that the life of a pastor should always be up! That would be a wrong conclusion.

We planted one church and assisted with a second. Pastorates took us to Minnesota, Nebraska, Florida, Washington State, and British Columbia, Canada. I would not lament any of our places of ministry because it was clear that God blessed and had a purpose in each place. Learning to adapt is just what we had to do. Being away from our parents, our children's grandparents, and our families during the kids' growing-up years was difficult. Yet, it is what we do.

Being a pastor's wife is difficult even in the best of times. Moving our family from one place to another over our years of pastoring was probably the hardest on our children. When the children suffer Momma suffers. However, when it came down to my pastor husband getting the axe, I understood a deeper suffering that still brings tears to my eyes. When I think of what he was feeling and what happened during the two years with no job or income, living in a country not our own, I ache. There was no way to defend ourselves within the intense calling nor was there a release from that call. You stand there and take the grit like a soldier, choosing how to act and as much as possible, choosing not to react.

It does no good to deny the damaged emotions that ensue or to go deep into disillusionment. It would only be destructive. And the enemy of our souls would win. Learning the painful lessons in the process of becoming overcomers and grace-filled forgivers is what this book is about.

Could we expect resolution or reconciliation to ever happen? The wait was difficult to say the least.

This is my story of our last church ministry and how God recycled our pain to transform us from being crippled Mephibosheths into agents of healing and help. It is my story about God's miraculous provision for every need during our pit time.

My prayer is that as you read this you will be a prayerful warrior for your pastor and family. The battle is fierce in these last days. I am not sure people in the body of Christ understand the intensity of the skirmishes and conflict, nor the commitment a vigorous schedule requires, and the perpetual emotional scope of the calling. I liken it to the circus acrobat who keeps multiple plates spinning on poles. The only difference is that in the pastorate the demands are around the clock for years on end. Find ways to bless your pastor and family, ways to love them and let them know of your support even though they are imperfect people.

"Appreciate your pastoral leaders who gave you the Word of God. Take a good look at the way they live, and let their faithfulness instruct you, as well as their truthfulness. There should be a consistency that runs through us all. For Jesus doesn't change—yesterday, today, tomorrow, He's always totally himself." (Hebrews 13:7-8, *MSG*)

This story is for my family and for generations to come: Listen dear kids, grandkids and great grandkids yet to come! Pull up a chair and give ear to what I want you to know. I'm chewing on what God has taught me and I'll let you in on the sweet old truths of the Word and of His goodness and provision in our lives. Stories I heard from my father and grandfather, guidance I learned at my mother's knee. I'm not keeping this to myself—I'm passing this story along to the next generations. It's about God's eminence, opulent riches and abundant provision. The marvelous things He has done. Never forget the works of God. Tell it to your kids and grandkids! Understand the truth which is so confused these days, so that your children can trust in God. (my paraphrase of Psalm 78:1-6)

God entered our story—to astound us and to transform us into the new! We experienced the shattering blows which prepared and equipped us to be healed helpers for others on their journey. He doesn't waste our story of loss and pain. That's how good God is!

Dianne Esau Porter

From Friends

DIANNE IS A master weaver. In this, her story, she weaves with bold color her pain, her loss, and her confusion. She takes you into the pit of disappointment and betrayal. Alongside this story, she weaves the beautiful Words of Life from a multitude of Scriptures that have guided, soothed, and comforted in her wilderness experience. She also weaves the seasoned, wise words of many known and unknown authors who have traveled with her on her journey to forgiveness, restoration, hope and a joyous life.

Her husband, Rick, is lovingly woven into the fabric of her story as her story is so often Rick's story too, because they are one in marriage and one in ministry.

The weaving of this honest, gut-wrenching story draws you into the sorrow, the trial, the joys and blessings of a woman who lives her life sold out to Jesus Christ and anchored solidly on God's Word. God's great work in Dianne's heart is revealed as we see her grow in her acceptance of the unexplained, putting her trust in the good sovereign purposes and plans of God.

Dianne comes through her story a different person in character, perseverance and hope. She wants us to learn from her and with her—and learn we will.

We painfully left our church just a few miles down the road from Rick and Dianne's church into a wilderness of loss, pain and confusion. There is no pain that is as confusing and messy as this pain. For a number of years, Rick and Dianne were our own faithful, caring pastor couple and fellow soul sojourners.

Under their honest and God-anointed ministry, we found the beginning of our own healing, hope and restoration. We have been blessed with their ministry, and now with Dianne's telling of the grief of their own painful church conclusion that is seldom understood unless experienced. She, along with us, has experienced the joy of journeying with other hurting pastor couples.

Thank you, dear Dianne, for taking the time to pour out your soul for us to learn from you and to walk with you. *The Lord is good; when trouble comes He is the place to go. – Nahum 1:7*

Pete and Shirley Unrau

Founders and Former Directors, OASIS Retreats of Canada

CHAPTER 1

Ambushed...By God

We don't know what to do; we're looking to you (God).

—II Chronicles 20:12, MSG

"Your beautifully messy complicated story matters (tell it)." This was the sentiment by author and artist Kelly Rae Roberts on a beautifully painted wall hanging my sister gave me last Christmas. I knew telling my story would be therapeutic and healing for me. Beauty can be revealed through painful stories of brokenness. Besides, I wanted my children, grandchildren and future generations to know of God's faithfulness in every part of my life. Even in the messy difficult times. We can always trust that God is Sovereign and knows what He is doing—all the time!

On January 5, 2004 my husband Rick was preaching with renewed vision and passion at the outset of a brand new year at our church in British Columbia. His text was from Numbers 10:29-32. Moses spoke to his father-in-law, "Come with us; we'll treat you well. God has promised good things for Israel. Come with me; we will go into the future with things God has prepared and promised for us. If you come with us, we'll make sure that you share in all the good things God will do for us."

This had been our church home for the last eight and one-half years and God had demonstrated many amazing miracles. Rick had led with perseverance and I believed, effectiveness. A few weeks before, we had been given a multi-page list of our shortcomings and things the elders deemed wrong with Rick's leadership. This had come out of nowhere and was quite a surprise to us. Yet, Rick's call from God was clear in him and he did not feel any release of that call after reading the document. So we persevered and asked for God's grace and strength to march on as His servants. Determined, we thought we could pray through it and keep the plates spinning! In a church of this size there were a lot of plates to spin at once and many hats to wear. Within a few weeks, our resignation was sought and Rick immediately submitted his letter even though it grieved us deeply to do so.

It didn't seem right to us. We felt ambushed! Our dreams died! Sometimes the hardest dreams to relinquish are our dreams for those we love. Our church family of almost nine years was lost—a job, friendships, hopes and routines. Our lives were disrupted with the isolation and uncertainty. How could we ever untangle the web of "whys" that haunted us?

When a loss hits in a sudden way there is no time to prepare. We were blindsided, caught off guard. We were headed in one direction and in an instant, totally unexpectedly, we were directionless. We wanted to hold on to the impression that we were in control of our lives. The ideal life was not happening in the way we had hoped.

As Jerry Sittser, a man who has persevered through much loss, suggests about such losses, it can feel like an amputation of one's identity. I believed Colossians 4:17: "See to it that you complete the work you have received in the Lord." Now what? We would not be able to complete it. Frederick Buechner wrote, "The place God calls you is the place where your deep gladness and the world's deep hunger meet, an honor and privilege from God with eternal ramifications." Rory Noland expresses the depth of call, "People called of God serve because it is a priority in their lives and it energizes them. They calculate the cost, but also see the benefits." We were not ready to leave the flock prematurely.

This was a totally new experience for us. It is safe to say that all of our previous ministries had been characterized by success, both apparent and real. Would life ever be the same? We now had to adapt to new circumstances. We so needed to call on God to forge a new identity, for God to grow us more and more to become persons whose worth is based on grace and not performance. Life as we knew it as a lead pastor for almost all the years of our marriage seemed abruptly ended. The video of our life froze as if a snapshot. We might one day redeem the loss, but it could not be reversed. We had never even sought a church to serve in our life. The opportunities came to us, doors wide open, as God willed and guided to our next place of service and ministry.

Now, self-doubt and self-pity paralyzed us; we were confused. We felt rejected, shelved, misunderstood, blamed, abandoned and disillusioned. Feeling like failed, cracked vessels. Rick's feelings of failure drained him of any ministry vision that was left in him.

As the questions tumbled around in my mind, I happened to read a devotional book days later. The February 1 entry in *Streams in the Desert* says, "This is my (God's) doing." (I Kings 12:24) Wow! That thought seemed like a preposterous impossibility to me! "My child, I have a message for you today. Let me whisper it in your ear so any storm clouds that may arise will shine with glory and the rough places you may have to walk will be made smooth. It is only four words, but let them sink into your inner being and use them as a pillow to rest your weary head. *This is my doing*. Have you realized that whatever concerns you, concerns Me too? ...You are precious and honored in my sight. (Isaiah 43:4) Therefore, it is my special delight to teach you…I am the God of circumstances. You did not come to this place by accident; you are exactly where I meant for you to be...Have you longed to do some great work for me, but instead have been set aside? ...The pain will leave as you learn to see ME in all things." (Laura Barter Snow)

Then this poem ended the entry:

This is from me, the Savior said,
As bending low He kissed my brow,
For One who loves you thus has led.
Just rest in Me, be patient now,
Your Father knows you have need of this,
Though, why perhaps you cannot see—
Grieve not for things you've seemed to miss.

The thing I send is best for thee.
Then looking through my tears, I plead,
Dear Lord, forgive, I did not know,
It will not be hard since You do tread,
Each path before me here below.
And for my good this thing must be
His grace sufficient for each test.
So still I'll sing, Whatever be
God's way for me is always best.

Was this really of God? How could this possibly be for our best? It seemed cruel and out of the blue. The enemy wants us to believe the lie that our wounding and struggles were out of God's *cruelty*. Does God allow this test so we can understand the potential God has placed within us to depend more on Him? In order for us to grow into our full potential in spiritual awareness and character development we may encounter trials and tests. Many and various! If we believe the lie of God's cruelty, it cuts us off from accepting *whose* we are and understanding *who* we are in Christ. I knew that this was somehow for my good, but I was not believing it in my heart.

I also had read that when you don't know what to do during the storm, keep your eyes on Jesus.

II Chronicles 20:12 describes such a situation: "We do not know what to do, but our eyes are upon You." The context is that of King Jehoshaphat realizing that he had no power to face the vast armies that were attacking him and his people. All the men of Judah and their wives and children stood there before the Lord, assembled in their great distress at Jerusalem's Temple of God. Thousands of families from near and far stood with Jehoshaphat imploring God's help and he ordered a nationwide fast. The country was unified. Jehoshaphat said, "When the worst happens—whether war or flood or disease or famine (insert *your* own worst)—and we take our place before the Temple (we know you are personally present in this place) and pray out our pain and trouble, we know that you will listen and give victory."

"Jahaziel was moved by God's Spirit to speak from the midst of this great unified people of Judah… Attention everyone…God's word: Don't be afraid; don't pay any mind to this vandal horde. This is God's war, not yours. Tomorrow you'll go after them…You won't have to lift a hand in this battle; just stand firm and watch God's saving work for you take shape. Don't be afraid, don't waver. March out boldly tomorrow—God is with you." (II Chronicles 20:14-17, *MSG*) Then "they praised at the top of their lungs!" (verse 19, *MSG*) Read about the surprise ending to this story in the remainder of that chapter. It is an amusing end of the story, but incredibly powerful. Could I have that kind of faith and strength for my new battle?

Did you know that this passage from II Chronicles contains the very middle verse of the entire Old Testament? There is a significant message in this center verse. "This is what the Lord says to you: Do not be afraid or discouraged because of this vast army. For the battle is not yours, but God's!" In the midst of the great victory, the people all sang loudly in praise to the Deliverer. They were a joyful choir of praise, an exuberant parade marching back to Jerusalem with sweet plunder! (verses 25 and 26) We dare not forget to praise God in the victories He grants us. Let's sing at the top of our lungs! That gives us peace and assurance that when we trust in God He will fight for us—if we don't shrink from our tasks in fear.

I could trust God with my own battle. As in I Peter 4:19 from *The Message*: "Trust him. He knows what he's doing, and he'll keep on doing it." God is completely dependable; He will not let me down. We may not understand the path God is allowing us to travel but the One who leads us knows the way. He will be with me and fight for me.

Rick preached his final Sunday at the church and between the two worship services, we literally ran to hide in the large baptistry behind the platform. We were never so thankful to be part of an immersing church! There was plenty of room! We were scared to death to engage anyone from the congregation and would not be able to say anything anyway. The truth could not be told that it was not by our choice that we were leaving. It all seemed surreal. I am not sure how they knew where we were hiding, but two city prayer warriors and friends not from our congregation found their way into the baptistry that day to be with us, pray for us and encourage us between services.

Our formal farewell was February 15, 2004. Done! Just like that. People in our congregation seemed to be as confused as we were. One individual asked, "Why are you running away from us?" The truth was not really being told and we were asked to be silent.

Our dear musician friends, Lori and Walter Funk and Dorita Smith, sang *Be Strong* at our farewell. The song was comforting though the lyrics lament that the castle falls, the heart breaks, hope is lost, the fears grow, the time flies, the road ends, a dream dies. Life goes on. Through it all we needed to be strong and not to be afraid. Take courage and fly! Taste the victory of grace! We were not alone in the world. We would stand, be strong, and walk in the Promised Land.

Our staff colleague, Pastor Rita, read Scripture passages at the farewell service that had so powerfully ministered to us through some dark circumstances in the previous months, "The God of all peace will soon crush Satan under your feet." (Romans 16:20) We later heard that a few elders were not appreciative of that word of Scripture and Pastor Rita was reprimanded.

A church staff member asked me on my quick get-away after our last service (as I ran to a side door behind the platform to a waiting car) if we had a church in Minnesota we were invited to pastor. Many of our colleagues had no idea what was suddenly happening.

CHAPTER 2

Isolation

But most days, I wander around feeling invisible. Like I'm a speck of dust floating in the air that can only be seen when a shaft of light hits it.

—Sonya Sones

Suddenly we were without a job or income, living in British Columbia so far from our families and all our children in the States. Our youngest daughter had attended Crown College in Minnesota and had just been married weeks before our "resignation." We felt the loneliness of living in isolation from those who meant the most to us. The separation felt almost like a death. The end of good relationships. Alone time and being cut off from so many allowed us time to wallow in our failure. Feeling flawed, defective, with a sense of disgrace. Despair forced our question of how long God would leave us in isolation and in our situation. It stripped us of our desires and dreams. Failure was always staring us in our face. We didn't want to be invisible but feeling shamed perpetuated the isolation. Hiding in safe numbness.

Loneliness and isolation came with a price for us. A life of abandon can be a minority life. Rick could not carry a cross in company. He could be surrounded by a crowd but his cross was his alone to carry; his carrying this cross set him apart. I feebly tried to help pick it up to help him carry it, but my assistance was shaky at best and ineffective. I was as wounded as he.

One of Rick's favorite books in this time was a dissertation by Shelley Trebesch (Barnabas Publishers) called *Isolation*. It is a small book on transformation in the life of a leader. Rick bought a number of these books to give away to other hurting ministry leaders. This book ministered deeply to Rick in isolation.

The two years before our departure had indeed been confusing and a spiritual conundrum to us, with what seemed like opposition of the enemy in every direction. In our post-departure isolation we remembered the confusing and amazing journey of our years at Sevenoaks Church.

The memories are vivid and unsettling. In December of 1995, within months of our arrival, a Christmas production was interrupted when one angel in the cast of twelve angels screamed out a blood-curdling cry. The angels stood on an A-frame structure behind a scrim. This happened as the baby Jesus was presented after His birth portrayal and as the wise men in all their regalia proceeded down the aisle to worship the Christ Child. The piercing scream, heard over the swelling music, stopped the entire production for some time. I was playing one of the keyboards and cannot remember a time in my life when I was so beyond petrified.

My daughter was the top angel on the scaffold and I thought perhaps someone had received an electrical shock from the excessive dry ice "smoke" condensing on bare feet near wiring. My daughter had told me that during one of the rehearsals the condensation was making the angels' feet burn so they had to imperceptibly move their feet to relieve the sensation of the burning cold. My music in the orchestra pit was being obscured by too-heavy smoke, more than was intended. At the direction of the conductor I was instructed to continue playing. The style was ethereal, the volume fortissimo. All the while I presumed something terrible had just happened. I could not focus because I was so afraid, yet somehow I persisted. The thought entered my mind that perhaps someone had been electrocuted.

An elder was working backstage. Rick ran to the back of the platform set to assess the situation. Later he made a brief announcement to assure the gathered crowd. The elder later indicated to Rick that the situation "appeared demonic." The girl angel who fell from her place did not remember a thing that happened. She did not know she had screamed.

She kept denying what was obvious to the other "angels." Right at the point of baby Jesus being birthed and presented! Approximately two thousand attendees witnessed the incident that third night Christmas performance. It seemed like forever that I continued improvising some keyboard orchestral chords as we waited to hear what had happened. I kept asking the director if he thought it was my Nikki that screamed or fell, but he wasn't saying a word. He likely had no idea and was as petrified as I was.

I was so unsettled that I could not get to sleep that night. My heart raced for hours. I was that freaked. So, what was *that* about?

The next morning was Sunday and the final Christmas production was to be Sunday night. Because of all the sets in place for the production, we had the heavy theatrical curtains shut for the normal Sunday morning service. Noises and the sound of growling behind the curtain during the Sunday morning service became disturbing. I happened to be at the piano. Rick and the worship pastor, on the platform, kept hearing noises behind the curtain. Assuming there were junior highers on the loose, Rick sent our worship pastor, Steve, behind the curtain to see what was going on. He returned saying there was nothing behind the curtain. Strange growling sounds continued, so Rick himself went to the back of the platform during the service and found nothing as well. Those were the first manifestations of the demonic in our church that continued on occasion in various places in the sanctuary over many years.

Intercessors prayed and prayed. One group even wrote warfare Scriptures on little pieces of paper, rolled them up into tiny bits and placed them in cracks in church walls where they would not be visible. Rick fasted when he would have to confront the demons in a conversation. Rick was confident in the finished and powerful work of Christ as he dealt with crazy stuff.

Some years after the angel incident, when one of the demonized individuals would puff up like the Incredible Hulk and lunge at Rick, he would speak in the authority of Christ to the demon and it would obey Christ in Rick, releasing the man gently back into his chair. One demon even identified himself by name to Rick as Molech. (Yet, Rick knew demons are liars too.) Not always did the demons inhabit a body. They were spirit but somehow would make their presence known around the church.

I could not wrap my mind around the demonic outbursts over the years. Worshippers in the front row with me one Sunday evening distinctly heard, "Porter, we hate you! We're going to kill you," in the most heinous voice. This happened after the demonized man had approached Rick up the steps to the pulpit. It appalled the lady sitting next to me, but I was no longer surprised by such outbursts. At that time Rick actually had a personal assistant who would act on Sundays as his body guard and that staff person ushered the man away from the pulpit.

I would lie awake at night trying to process the cacophony going on in my mind as to what God might be doing. Why was the powerful good news of the Gospel sometimes opposed in this particular place? Rick was a praying man and there were church prayer services many times a week, including area-wide prayer services held at our church. The blood of the Lamb and all the Scriptural tools of warfare were implemented and applied. We were not afraid. "Greater is He that is in us than he that is in the world." (I John 4:4) The Spirit in us was far stronger than anything in the world.

Among the difficult memories that flooded back during our isolation were those of teen suicides in the church. For these families, all of whom were dear to us, we grieved deeply. Officiating at memorial services for teens was not something anyone would want to do. Our entire city was affected by this. Counselors and local youth pastors began working in the city schools. How does one process the whys of this kind of loss?

I had dreams that I knew were from the Lord that didn't seem to make any sense at the time but later I would understand them. They were so heavy on my heart, and seemed to be prophetic from the Lord, that I would ask Rick for the interpretation. What did it mean? Sometimes he knew. Sometimes I knew. In one of my dreams the details were bewildering. It involved full overflowing toilets and the contents running down the inclined aisles of the church toward the platform that nobody saw except me. All were oblivious to it. I will spare all the details here. This time the interpretation came to me without inquiring: "Focus on the Father and not the feces!" Rick shared it as a sermon illustration the following Sunday. Not sure what folk thought about that! I don't blame them; I wasn't sure myself what to think. I was often confused!

These wild and crazy memories flooded back as we had time to ruminate and contemplate in the realization that our vision for the church and our dreams had died. It was finished.

Our farewell reception on Sunday afternoon, February 15, 2004 seemed thrown together and disorganized. We received heartfelt and loving notes and cards from many in the flock who were grieved to see us leave and didn't really understand what was happening. One such card I taped in my journal. This is what it said: "God bless those blessings in disguise. God speaks to us through toilet paper on shoes, runs in stockings, and life's humiliating experiences that keep us laughing at ourselves along the way. God speaks to us through long lines, and traffic jams, and all the annoying little inconveniences that make us slow down and take a deep breath. God speaks to us through flat tires, bounced checks, broken appliances, and all the little 'last straws' that make us say, 'I give up!' so He can finally take over." Then on the inside of the card was this sentiment, "Knock! Knock! Who's there? You know Who. Hold on tight—God is up to something wonderful for you." This card made me smile.

Another card was a Roy Lessin quote. "Just think! You're not here by chance but by God's choosing. His hand formed YOU and made you the person you are. He compares you to no one else—You are one of a kind. You lack nothing that His grace cannot give you. He has allowed you to be here at this time in history to fulfill His special PURPOSE for this generation." It continued with a verse from II Peter 1:4 and "in appreciation of your service in God's place at God's perfect time. Thank you! Thank you!" The long lines of well-wishers at the farewell blessed us in spite of the awkward situation. A cloud hung over our heads that didn't seem to lift even with wonderful people expressing their gratitude for our service.

Immediately after the farewell we took a trip to Boise, Idaho to visit our daughter Vonda and family for a few days to attempt to clear our confused minds and hurting souls. And, let's be honest, to get out of town. The drive over to Boise and time with family was good and therapeutic. Time with my, then, only grandson warmed the heart of this grandma too.

After our trip to Boise we found ourselves back at home in British Columbia in isolation and the unknown became our routine. I journaled that I felt sort of a mental and heart strangulation as time went on. We had never been quitters before. In fact Rick had a work ethic that cannot be rivaled. We would have moved away in a heartbeat if we had a job or place to go. As Jerry Sittser says in his book, *A Grace Disguised*, we felt "profound sadness…the disability is permanent. No therapy will alter the condition. One is suspended between a past for which we long and a future for which we hoped. The desire is to return to recover what we lost but instead the barren present is only memories of the past that only reminds us of what we lost...It takes time for past memories to comfort rather than torment."

Moving away would not help me deny or escape my feelings. The pain would haunt and chase me. Over time we needed to take stock of what we could learn through this and what we knew to be true about God. Nothing could separate us from the love of God. (Romans 8:38-39) His silence should not be mistaken as His indifference. II Corinthians 4:8-12 from *The Message*, assured me that troubles wouldn't defeat us and hurt could not destroy us. "We've been surrounded and battered by troubles, but we're not demoralized; we're not sure what to do, but we know that God knows what to do. We have been spiritually terrorized, but God hasn't left our side; we've been thrown down, but we haven't broken…Our lives are at constant risk for Jesus' sake, which makes Jesus' life all the more evident in us. While we're going through the worst, you're getting in on the best!"

Don't be afraid to tell God that your situation doesn't make sense or to tell Him exactly how you feel because He is big enough to handle it. Jerry Sittser says the God depicted in the Psalms is big enough to absorb our accusations and to take full responsibility for the suffering of the world. Being honest with God is not blasphemous. As a Christ follower,

I reasoned that I should never allow myself to have negative emotions, fear, anger or depression. It stigmatized me and seemed inappropriate to have these feelings because God is love and He grants us peace. I have wrestled with that. Yet the Psalms give us permission to ask our questions about suffering and wounding. The Psalms teach us the language of the soul. They are a model of how to ask questions of God without fear of compromising our relationship with Him or others.

I've read somewhere that lament is in 70% of the Psalms. Lament helps me be real—the language of lament is both a cry for help and an affirmation of underlying trust in God. Lament expresses weakness and desperation, but not utter hopelessness! Telling God the truth of how I feel is closer to godliness than pretending will ever be. Lament means to vent or complain. Refusal to settle for the way things are. Inquire of God. Don't pretend. Name the hurt. Emotions expose our cry of the sorrow in our soul and reveal what our heart is doing with God in the battle. Tell Him you need help!

Psalm 142, verses 1 and 4, are a desperate prayer of David in a cave where he found no escape. He was in deep trouble. He called out in something akin to a scream, asking God, "How long will you hide your face from me? How long before you will do justice?" A desperate time pushes us to ask the Lord to *do something* for us! No pain feels light or momentary when you are in its grip. God told David to get up off his lament and go! Stand! David then strengthened himself with trust in his God. (I Samuel 30:6) He still had more questions after "strengthening himself in the Lord." God became his trusty ally and deliverer in great battles. David is a model for us to scream our pain and then to strengthen ourselves in the Lord. Walter Brueggemann, quoted in *Cry of the Soul* by Dan Allender, reminds us that no situation falls outside of Yahweh's capacity for transformation.

Psalm 22 is also a frame of David's expression of intense pain, distress and anguish. The telling of his experiences is compared to torment, physical weakness, complete helplessness, and the suspense of waiting on God to deliver him. God's silence became a problem for David.

The details are gripping. He likens his tormentors to masses of howling beasts attempting to devour him, gnawing at his hands and feet.

Yet David's resilience in his reliance on God consisted of praising God for His glory and faithfulness. He affirmed that God had not failed to help those who trusted Him in previous generations. *The Message* is so descriptive! Read to the end of chapter 22. David ended up gathering his people (verses 25-31) for worship to discover the praise-life. "Down-and-outers sit at God's table and eat their fill. Everyone on the hunt for God is here, praising Him. Live it up, from head to toe. Don't ever quit." The Psalms teach us how to praise and worship, but they also teach us how to wrestle with doubt until it gives way to the first glimmers of hope.

One of the most wonderful aspects of our relationship with Christ is that we don't necessarily *have* to talk or scream. He understands my exhausting pain without my even having to voice it. Trying to explain our pain to others and how we feel is arduous. "What a relief it is to be able to lay down in a field with the Shepherd and not have to say a word." (Sheila Walsh) He is a Man of Sorrows, acquainted with grief. "When all kinds of trials crowd into your lives, my friends, don't resent them as intruders but welcome them as friends." (James 1:2, *Phillips*) Acknowledge that Christ is Lord even in the trials of hurt and loss.

It is good to know that the Spirit himself groans on my behalf as I groan what I cannot express in words. The moment we get tired in the waiting, God's Spirit is right alongside helping us. If we don't know how or what to pray, it doesn't matter. He does our praying in and for us, making prayer out of our wordless sighs, our aching groans. He knows us far better than we know ourselves, knows our condition, and keeps us present before God.

Chuck Swindoll in *Hope Again* offers some good insight on various forms of trials we experience. The word *various* (as in numerous and different forms of trials) comes from the Greek term *poikolos* which means variegated or many-colored. He writes, "Trials come in many forms and colors. They are different, just as we are different. Something that would hardly affect someone else might knock the slats out from under me.

But God offers special grace to match every shade of sorrow." I like that—every shade of sorrow and how we react to the trial is different.

At first I couldn't and didn't know how to pray into our situation other than reading and praying the Psalms. I had to actually read my prayers taken from a little book called *Wounded Hearts Renewed Hope* by Michelle McKinney Hammond (Harvest House Publishers). My sister-in-law sent me the book at just the right time. The published prayers beautifully prayed my heart's cry to God when I couldn't even find the words. Hammond addressed the wounded heart and admitted her struggle with unforgiveness—the inability to let go. Wondering if she'd ever recover, ever trust again, begin again, and be able to move on. The book was an amazing gift at just the right time!

We did not just stew in our isolation. We traveled some. Rick also worked on our house in preparation for a sale in some unknown future. He also tried a few doors of possible future employment or education, but all of them seemed locked. Meanwhile, I was surprised how deeply we felt betrayal, disillusioned by what we perceived God was doing only to be rejected and left in total disarray and confusion. My mind was in turmoil and I was stuck, not understanding what was going on, why it happened or how this could possibly be in God's plan. My brain tried to over-process our situation. I was only drawing on what I was depositing in my memory bank, and that was not good. My racing mind often would not allow me to sleep well at night. Constant repetition of thoughts only fertilized the negativity. How could mulling it over any more in my mind help the situation?

Chants of conundrums were caged inside of me causing confusion. I had not yet taken the advice of II Corinthians 10:5 from the King James Version, "Casting down imaginations, and every high thing that exalts itself against the knowledge of God, and bringing into captivity every thought to the obedience of Christ." I should have refused to let my emotions and feelings satisfy or dominate my mind; we tend to become what we think. I knew that this spirit, operating in my mind, would make me weaker. I knew I needed to decree that no weapon formed against me would be able to prosper and God had promised to show wrong every tongue that rose against me. Isaiah 54:17 declares that this vindication is from the Lord.

I have trouble letting things go. I somehow had the misconception that if I would run over the details of my conundrum in my head just a few more times, it would somehow change the outcome and I might then be able to uncover some *new* understanding of the situation. How or where could I get another opinion? Foolish, really.

The longer we waited on some answer, the more I became bitter. After all, I knew exactly how terribly hard my husband had worked to the point of exhaustion, physically and mentally, all the time. Whatever hurt him hurt me. In my perception, he had sweat blood and had hung on the cross for this church body. Did anyone else understand that? Rick labored with his whole heart, leaving no part of his heart behind him. God does not give harvests to idle men. Did anyone know how much I had to give up my husband and his time and gifts to the body of Christ? Wasn't that a huge sacrifice? I was away from my older children, parents and siblings, serving in a country not my own. After years of strong effective leadership and spiritual insights and sensitive wisdom in serving this large church, Rick absolutely did not deserve this! Because he was in pain, feeling worthless and rejected, I agonized even more for him. I literally became physically ill. Pain seemed to consume and be magnified in my focus, rather than trusting Almighty Sovereign God.

Are we not prone to dwell more on anxieties, difficulties, and bruised egos, than God's wonders and mysteries? I knew in my heart that no problem was greater than His strength. "You hold strength and power in the palm of your hand to build up and strengthen all." (I Chronicles 29:12, *MSG*) The battle expressed in Ephesians 6:10 in *The Message* spoke to me of how to equip myself: "Fight to the finish. Be prepared. You're up against far more than you can handle on your own. Take all the help you can get, every weapon God has issued, so that when it's all over but the shouting you'll still be on your feet." After all, there is no fragrance without crushing the flowers, no wine without pressing the grapes, no oil without squeezing the olives and no real joy without the sorrow.

God has entrusted a huge assignment to pastors—the spiritual well-being of His flock. Now if the Shepherd wasn't there to lie across the gate of the sheep fold, who would protect the flock from outside marauders? My journal contains this observation of an author whose name I did not record, "When deep desires, God's call, and obstacles collide the result is intense emotions, confusion, hopelessness, rejection, anger, frustration and pain." We were expected to have ideal families, to be perfect people, to always be available, to never be down and to have all the answers. We needed to keep our own lives stable and moving forward in addition to guiding and supporting the lives of others. These expectations are unrealistic, yet most people are disappointed when a pastor becomes overwhelmed, seems depressed, lets us down in some way, or completely burns out. Moreover, if the pastor ever tells the truth about it, watch out. Most churches don't know what to do with a leader in any level of crisis who shares authentically from that crisis.

Charles Spurgeon, in *Letters to My Students*, (Zondervan, pp. 158-162), wrote "Let no man who looks for ease of mind and seeks the quietude of life enter the ministry; if he does so he will flee from it in disgust." We had known the high cost of serving many churches, east coast to west coast of North America, in our lifetime. We also knew His grace through it all.

J. Oswald Sanders expressed my thoughts exactly: "No one need aspire to leadership in the work of God who is not prepared to pay a price greater than his contemporaries and colleagues are willing to pay. True leadership always extracts a heavy toll on the whole man, and the more effective the leadership is, the higher the price to be paid."

Rick was driven by intense passion and he felt issues deeply. He was careful, however, to hear from God as to how to guide the flock into truth. God's Spirit miraculously bore witness with Rick's spirit as to how to speak, counsel, guide, attend, lead, advise, warn, and declare the whole counsel of God.

I recalled a recent new friend in our church, another pastor's wife in our city, who told me she and her pastor husband were now a part of our church for a time of healing since their devastating removal from their own church in our town. She related that it was the most painful, wounding experience she and her husband had ever gone through in their entire life. Much more devastating and difficult than her diagnosis of potentially terminal cancer, she related. Some years later she made this statement to her former church leader regarding her pain: "This crisis in our church is more painful to me than my six and one half hours of cancer surgery. The doctor had told us it was the fastest and deadliest of all cancers and he didn't know if he could save my life. So facing terminal cancer was very real, but I was focusing on the actual PAIN of the *big surgery*." This new friend was a sweet, strong, mature woman of God, older than I and stronger in her faith, a warrior in prayer. I remember at the time wondering how that much pain could be possible in losing a church involuntarily...until now. She and her husband had recently founded and administered Oasis Retreats across Canada for hurting pastors, spouses and ministry leaders. They were gifted in loving, understanding, counseling and mercy giving. This couple cared for us in so many ways, having walked the same road. At the time, I did not fully understand the depth of pain she expressed to me until it happened to us. That brought new perspective!

These words in my journal were written out of empathy for Rick. "I have preached You to the whole congregation. I have kept back nothing, God. You know that! I didn't keep the news of your ways as a secret, didn't keep it to myself. I told it all, how dependable you are, how thorough. I didn't hold back the pieces of love and truth for myself alone. I told it all... let the congregation know the whole story. NOW GOD, don't hold out on me, don't hold back your compassion. Your love and truth are all that keeps me together." (Psalm 40:9-11)

Sometimes I wondered if maybe Rick was perceived to be too passionate about Jesus and in pursuit of perpetual prayer, aspiring and believing for too much within the Bride of Christ. Telling it all as Psalm 40 revealed! He had deeper faith than anyone I had met. Was this mistaken for fantasy? Should he have been more measured? Did this put a few leaders on edge? How can one mute a passion, especially if it is understood to be driven by God Himself? Should it be suppressed in favor of public opinion? He has always followed Christ with wild abandon, quietly fearless with determination and constancy even in the face of difficult circumstances. Others in our church and city who were sensitive to the Spirit would confirm to Rick exactly what He was hearing from God and affirm his leading that would ensue, sometimes in mysterious ways. In retrospect, Rick agrees that he probably spoke too openly about God's leading and was often too sure of prophetic intimations, revealing them when perhaps they were really intended for his own personal prayer life. He was impeccably truthful and vulnerable in his preaching. Many people liked that about him. What you see is what you get! Rick owns all that and considers it a lesson learned.

Many people, sometimes through tears, communicated with Rick that they were growing by leaps and bounds in their faith. The miraculous was evident. The shepherd of the flock was hearing from the Spirit and following the Good Shepherd. I was confident of that. Rick is one who knows the times and what God is trying to communicate (or even shout) to the people in these seasons and times. Rick would say it with controlled abandon. Sometimes it would be resisted. Sometimes it would be resoundingly received.

Rick was preaching through the seven churches of Revelation. When he got to the Church at Sardis, the church that had the reputation for vigor and zest, but they were asleep—stone dead, Rick felt compelled that Sunday to shout, "Wake Up!" over the church. Shouting didn't go over well that day according to a few folk and Rick received communications that implied the church *was* fully awake and alive and did not need to be reminded to be roused from their sleep and complacency or to wake up.

Yet, a professor at Trinity Western University who attended our church had written an email to Rick a day or two before that Sunday. Her email said, "Rick, you are unsettled about whether you should do something on Sunday morning. You are to go ahead and do as the Lord told you." She had no idea what that *thing* was. Indeed, Rick had been uncomfortable about it. When Rick did shout "Wake up" that day after affirmation that he perceived to be from God, it didn't fall well on the ears of some people. Actually, the recording of the message that day had three echoes reverberating for each time he shouted, "Wake up!" Hmm, a bit mysterious! Sounded like it was echoing from the mountaintops!

Then the questions set in. Rick wondered if he *really* heard from God. Had it *really* been confirmed by the professor's email, or was he just straining under the pressures of life and leadership? A few days after the "wake up" shout, he received another confirmation. A local pastor called. "I heard you shouted 'wake up' in your sermon Sunday. I just wanted you to know that I had a call from Texas. A pastor there in our church network felt led to tell me that God had a message for Abbotsford. 'Wake up!'"

As Revelation 3:2-3 says, "*Wake up*! Get up on your feet! Strengthen what remains and is about to die, for I have found your deeds unfinished in the sight of my God. Remember, therefore, what you have received and heard; hold it fast, and repent. But if you do not wake up, I will come like a thief and you will not know at what time I will come to you...If you pull the covers back over your head and sleep on, oblivious to God, I'll return when you least expect it." God doesn't want or need our busy work in which none of it is actually His work. But He does want us to get up on our feet! Listen "to the Wind Words, the Spirit blowing through the churches." (Revelation 3:6, *MSG*)

We can find joy and wonderful surprise in our moments as we remain disciplined to stay awake to God's presence. Be watchful of what God does. Be awake to and aware of God as a loving Father who gives us a quality of life—sustained every moment of life in being alert and responsive to God's love and care. It will go well with us whom the Master finds wide awake on His return. Ephesians 5:15-17 in *The Message* tells us to "Wake up from your sleep. Climb out of your coffins; Christ will show you the light! So watch your step. Use your head. Make the most of every chance you get. These are desperate times! Don't live carelessly, unthinkingly."

A few took issue when Rick preached "holiness" as well. It was obvious to me that you can't study the Bible earnestly and attentively without missing an obvious fact that personal holiness is exceedingly important to God. Are we too afraid of holiness, of mystery; are we numbed to the sensation of *wonder*? "We live in a time when faith is thin, because our aching for what is above and beyond us has been anaesthetized and our capacity for wonder reduced to clever tricks." (Alan Jones, *Passion for Pilgrimage*) I also like what A. W. Tozer said a long time ago: "Culture is putting out the light in men and women's souls." He is right. Should we not long for a faith that is considered dangerous and risky as contrasted to our predictable, rebellious, defiant, and entitled mentality?

Christian maturity and holiness are on display in Colossians 1:28: "He is the one we proclaim, admonishing and teaching everyone with all wisdom, so that we may present everyone fully mature in Christ." In Eugene Peterson's *Leap Over a Wall* he writes of reflections on spirituality from the life of David. He says there is a difference between growth and change, but both are valued. "When we grow, in contrast to merely change, we venture into new territory and include more people in our lives—serve more and love more. Our culture is filled with change; it's poor in growth. New things, models, developments, opportunities are breathlessly announced every hour. But instead of becoming ingredients in a long and wise growth, they simply replace. The previous is discarded and the immediate stuck in—until, bored by the novelty, we run after the next fad. Men and women drawn always to the new never grow up. God's way is growth, not change."

Are we losing growth and holiness? I am concerned that we are. We are so caught up in the idolatry of the novelty—entertainment, latest movies we must see in order to critique our latest opinions on social media, the latest in fashion—novelty even in the church and in business. We hop from one thing to the next in order to stay interested, but never really growing in the process. Getting stimulated but never going deep, as Peterson suggests. John Maxwell captured this when he said, "Change is inevitable. Growth is optional."

These considerations bombarded my thoughts as I contemplated our last years at Sevenoaks. In isolation there is plenty of time to remember.

In our alone, dark time we were comforted: "Turn to me and be gracious to me, for I am lonely and afflicted." (Psalm 25:16) We needed someone to hold us and tell us everything would be OK. The sea of people all around us could not be perceived in our isolation. Rick ordered that book entitled *Isolation* so we could gain understanding in the dark what needed to happen down the road in the light. God continued to love us in our isolation. "God has infinite attention to spare for each one of us. You are as much alone with Him as if you were the only being He had ever created." (C. S. Lewis) This thought was a comfort to us. We were always on His mind.

CHAPTER 3

Oasis

What makes the desert incredible and intriguing, bearable and beautiful for me, is that somewhere it conceals an oasis.

—*Dianne Porter*

After our requested resignation, the church board was asked if they would fund an Oasis Retreat (oasisretreatscanada.com) for us. They agreed. As I said, this is a wonderful retreat for hurting ministry couples administered at that time by our friends, Pete and Shirley Unrau, and offered by Campus Crusade for Christ Canada (now called Power to Change). Rick had been a presenter/speaker at Oasis Retreats on several occasions. What a surprise when we became attendees. Going from large church lead pastor and presenter to wounded participant in the same retreat was quite an adjustment, and a healthy one in spite of the pain.

Soon after our return from visiting Boise, off we drove to the little town called Hope, British Columbia. I hopped out of the car to take a photo of the Hope sign. Was it a sign of hope from God? Indeed it was! The retreat ministered hope in Hope. We received the loving guidance of professional Christian counselors to help us understand we were not alone in our situation. We reviewed our Birkman personality inventories for clarity and understanding, assisted by a certified leader to interpret them for us. He explained how each of us ticks, both separately and together as a pastoral couple team. The retreat was also enriched by times of worship in which we could sing out our pain to God. We were served and cared for.

We listened to wonderful speakers who knew how to touch and salve our hurt. All this in a context of good food and new friends.

Our amazing, internationally-known counselor, Dr. John Radford, from Vancouver (originally from South Africa, with years of experience in reconciliation including involvement in the post-apartheid healing in his homeland), helped us at the retreat and through the next many months with loving and prayerful counseling sessions. What a gift! He would continue after the retreat to accompany and companion us into unfamiliar territory. The only problem was, we had attended this Oasis Retreat at a time when our pain was so new, fresh and huge that it was difficult to absorb all that was being shared with us. In addition, I was so physically weak and sick that I was distracted by insomnia, bronchitis, asthma, coughing and reluctantly went home a day early from our week-long gathering. I went directly to the doctor.

Our friend, composer, worship leader and recording artist, Brian Doerksen, wrote an email saying he'd come over with his guitar and sing the love of the Father over us. He lived close to our home. Another friend actually cared! One song on his CD, *Today*, became one of our theme songs. It was "Lead Us Lord" and on several occasions he sang it over us. The lyrics affirmed, "Here we stand at a crossroads again; like you said in time the seasons change. Looking back we recall the blessing and the pain, but now we turn our hearts toward what is still to come. We want to dream again. Lead us Lord into a life of fruitfulness. Prepare our hearts to risk again. As we trust, taking simple steps of obedience, we know that you will lead us, Lord." (Used with permission—briandoerksen.com) In fact, Brian dedicated that album to us in the CD notes: "Rick and Diane Porter (he misspelled my name): This one is especially for you! You have been a Nehemiah leader in our city!"

"This is what God says: Stand at the *crossroads* and look; ask for the ancient paths (the tried and true godly path), ask where the good way is, and walk in it, and you will find rest for your souls." (Jeremiah 6:16) An oasis! We acknowledged, here we are Lord at the crossroads! Lead us, Lord! "Show me your ways, O Lord, teach me your paths; guide me in your truth and teach me, for you are God my Savior, and my hope is in you all the day long." (Psalm 25:4-5)

Other treasured songs from Brian's pen were *Faithful One, Your Faithfulness*, and *You Shine*. Music ministered deeply to my heart during these trying days. Songs became my comfort, giving me strength and encouragement. Yet, all I could see in my desert were the cactuses, tumbleweeds, thistles and endless sand. I could see little else, hear nothing. We were solitary pilgrims in the desert in search of an oasis. The vastness of the open spaces left me no place to hide or find refuge. Lead us, Lord through the desolation and vast horizon that seems to never end to find refuge in You.

CHAPTER 4

One Grand Gift

God will reach to the last grain of sand and the remotest star to bless us if we will only obey Him...He is our source. As the psalmist said, "All my springs of joy are in You." (Psalm 87:7, NASB)

–Oswald Chambers from My Utmost for His Highest

Isolation also invited some wonderful memories. It wasn't all demons and disaster. From time to time we remembered the amazing things God had done at Sevenoaks Church even though all did not end well. One miracle beyond what we could have ever dreamed to the glory of God was what was called "One Grand Gift." I had been reviewing and remembering with a full heart what God had done in our church over the early years we were there. God was moving in mysterious, miraculous ways that we could hardly grasp.

The pain of the present became a good time to remember former days when our faith and trust in God were being bolstered, augmented, and reinforced. People's lives were being changed dramatically. Stories abounded. These past miracles were part of what made the present pain especially difficult to understand and accept. There *had* been good times!

When we arrived in Abbotsford, we came to a church with debt approaching two million dollars on the building. Rick concluded it would be something that he would address with the board early on. The newest part of the church, a sanctuary that seated 2,400, had a debt from the time it was built 15 years previous to our arrival. There had been ill-feeling regarding the debt in previous years and a sense that the leaders had overspent their borrowing authority. The debt was greater than it should be and had been hanging over the church ministry for too long.

The people had little desire to address the situation. There seemed to be a lack of participation in giving with some congregants. The previous pastor, the Rev. Al Runge, had successfully completed a few efforts toward reducing the debt by a few hundred thousand dollars. But there seemed to be a cessation of participation for various reasons. Worse yet, the debt became an easy excuse for maintaining the status quo. After Rick had been at the church one year, our worship pastor announced that he would be resigning and moving on. This was a significant loss. It seemed then that we needed a project and challenge.

Rick happened to be talking with a friend, Scottie May, who told Rick how her church, then known as Blanchard Road Alliance Church in Wheaton, Illinois, eliminated a large debt in a single offering. She described the miracle of it all. Inspired by her story, Rick went to the board with an idea in the early summer of 1996. He proposed a campaign to move toward collecting a single offering to eliminate the debt. The board appreciated Rick's vision, but had better awareness of past efforts that failed, not to mention the latest ill feelings. Some were hesitant. One said it couldn't be done—they had tried before. Rick's only fear was that not only was the project daunting and risky, it was early in his tenure to set himself up for a big failure. Maybe smaller projects would be a better idea.

Yet in consultation with the board it was concluded that it would be good to plan this for the end of the year to maximize year-end giving for tax purposes. This would also permit people to bridge their gift across two calendar years.

Someone came up with the name "One Grand Gift" for the campaign and they began to focus on a single cash offering scheduled for December 21, 1996. This required faith! Huge faith! The offering would be received at Christmas time. Thus, the "gift" idea was incorporated. God gave His best gift in the season we celebrate as Christmas. Could we not give out of the fullness of our hearts?

There was no shortage of complaint that a giving emphasis during the holiday season was not a good idea. Every December our church was known for its dramatic Christmas productions which cost quite a chunk of money. The concerts were billed as an outreach of the church to our community and all the way to Vancouver. People came expecting quality drama and music productions every year with all the bells and whistles. It *was* good and there was a reputation among the music and acting community. I had enjoyed participating musically in these productions. This capital campaign in the middle of these multiple productions offered to thousands of people at no cost would stretch the resources of the church.

Once the date was set to receive the offering, leaders began to challenge the congregation toward full participation cheerfully and not under compulsion. There were approximately 1,000 households in the church. As the day approached some of the older members shared their stories. They told of how their faith had led to provision of funds that enabled them to give gifts, some large, in previous campaigns. With the leadership of the church staff, participation was encouraged for all age levels. From little ones on up to the eldest! The kids went to work on their projects. By the time we began to print materials, it was estimated that the principal due as of January 1, 1997 would be $1,350,000. What a goal! Nearly one and one-half million dollars! The elders and Rick defined three goal levels. In this way, the (nervous) pastor covered himself if the effort fell short, so we could still claim victory. Rick said his faith was small initially; he was afraid of failure. He did some "feigning" of faith, hiding his knocking knees behind the pulpit.

In late fall Rick received a note card with a check enclosed. It was from a young professional woman in church who had been stricken with a debilitating disease. She was ultimately confined to a wheelchair. She had not been able to work and she had little or no income. In the note she shared that God had led her specifically to send an early faith gift of $200. Rick was surprised to receive an early gift because all the promotional materials declared that December 21 was the focus date for the one-time cash offering.

Later we learned the "rest of the story." This woman had written the check and was preparing to mail it at God's direction even though she did not have the money on hand. That day she went to the mailbox and found a gift of $200 from a friend. The Lord covered her check before He asked her to send it. This gift became to Rick the foundation for faith for this one-time offering. He saw it as God's earnest money. Rick's faith grew. He rested in the peace that God was in this. This relatively small gift was a first fruit, a Biblical concept of a small initial harvest representing the entire harvest. It was like the boy's little lunch that fed 5,000, or the widow's mite, which though small, was huge.

With this concept confirmed and Rick believing he was aligning his heart to God's heart, this challenge was as good as done in Rick's mind. It *could* be done! It *would* be done. Rick and others on the board and staff would have the faith to believe for a miracle. We believed this would strengthen the body of Christ as we had faith, knowing the first small gift was a sign from God that He would indeed supply.

A service of victory was planned for December 21. The choir prepared the *Hallelujah Chorus* to be sung at the end, among other songs, with confidence that the full amount would be given in cash that day. There were stations in aisles and in foyers around the church. Police officers in the congregation were prepared for any disruption. The exterior doors were locked for security. Then an entire march offering by all ages ensued. Exciting, exhilarating, electrifying! The children had wheelbarrows full of glistening coins (loonies and toonies—Canadian $1 and $2 coins) piled to the top of the wheelbarrows. They had given these in the weeks previous in various children's ministry venues. Kids excitedly skipped and pranced, following the offerings like a scene from The Pied Piper! These visuals and memories of God's grace and provision still are blazoned in my mind to this day.

Some elderly folk, usually unable to get out of their nursing homes, wanted to be there for the thrilling day. There were more wheelchairs than normal in church. Families wheeled elderly parents down the aisle so they could participate. The offering was received. Participation was astounding! Tears were streaming down faces! Others were praising the Lord as they marched.

The offering counters went off to tabulate the offering. Rick preached. I'm not sure if anyone was listening as we contemplated what God would do. After some time Rick inquired if any counters had returned to the service and had a number total for all of us. No counters were there. Someone shouted from the back that they were nowhere near done counting yet. So Rick went a bit longer, (this is one of his gifts!) and we waited.

Later another counter came back saying that it was going to be a while yet and the number was well over a million dollars at that point... and counting. Knowing many could not wait into the afternoon to learn the amount, Rick told the choir to go ahead and to sing the *Hallelujah Chorus* by faith. He said that our praise was to God and not just for an offering and hence the planned praise was appropriate regardless of the size of the offering. Sing they did! There was expectancy and electricity in the room.

It was late and Rick wasn't sure what to do, but decided to release the people to go home after the victory was already celebrated, with no certainty of the final numbers yet. We learned that afternoon that an offering of well over $1 million had been given but some people who were out of town that weekend indicated that they would give their gift upon their return. At the Christmas Eve services, three days later, we were able to announce that the total amount of the One Grand Gift had been miraculously met. In one offering, including pledges to be given immediately in the new year, the total was announced. $1,349,847! Over 900 households participated. Additional gifts were soon received to put the offering over the $1.35 million goal, and demonstrate again that God gives more than we ask! Praise the Lord! His wonders to perform (the song comes to mind)!

Psalm 34:10: ..."those who seek the Lord lack no good thing." Philippians 4:19: "And my God shall supply every need of yours according to His riches in glory in Christ Jesus." "The Lord is my Shepherd; I shall not want." (Psalm 23:1) "...put me to the test, says the Lord of hosts, if I will not open the windows of heaven for you and pour down for you a blessing until there is no more need." (Malachi 3:10)

This was the beginning of some miraculous endeavors that were happening at Sevenoaks Alliance Church in Abbotsford, British Columbia. To God be all the praise! To this day I have visuals displayed in my mind of all that we celebrated that day!

That was the beginning of the Nehemiah years—the building of the walls. Not just in Sevenoaks Church but in the churches of the city of Abbotsford as well. God was good! Community, cooperation, and prayerful partnering began to have a ripple effect.

CHAPTER 5

Nehemiah Years

Those laborers who were laden with the materials to rebuild the wall did their work with one hand supporting their load and one hand holding a weapon.

—Nehemiah 4:17, NLT

Nehemiah and his wall rebuilders of the temple in Jerusalem prayed because they were so despised and insulted. Sanballat and Tobiah along with the Arabs, Ammonites, and Ashdodites were furious that the repair was happening and the whole wall was soon to be joined together because "the people had a heart for the work." Because the walls were being fixed, the dissenters decided to fight and create as much opposition as they possibly could.

Nehemiah "stationed armed guards at the most vulnerable places on the wall," assigning families with weapons. Nehemiah even kept a trumpeter by his side to sound the alert. "There's a lot of work going on and we are spread out all along the wall, separated from each other. When you hear the trumpet call, join us there; our God will fight for us. And so we kept working, from first light until the stars came out, half of us holding lances." Fascinating story from Nehemiah Chapter 4 and following!

One huge passion of Rick's during our tenure in Canada had been prayer and city-wide praise, worship and a desire for revival in our city. This is what Brian Doerksen referred to when he dedicated his album *TODAY* to Rick and me, calling Rick the "Nehemiah city guy"—a passion to bring the city together in unity. A rebuilding of the city walls of sorts.

Brian had come to Rick's office early in 1999, not long after Rick had been elected to lead the ministerial association of our area, to assure Rick that he was on board for whatever God should call him to do to be a Nehemiah builder in our city. Brian likewise felt called to revival and to participate musically, prayerfully and in any way he could.

Brian had recently moved back to his home town of Abbotsford from England after composing, leading worship and recording there. He lived a short distance from our home. He was also an advocate for revival and building cooperation for community among the churches in our city. Intercessors in the area were with us in this as well. Many had interceded for years and longed for a builder and leader to prepare the way for God to move within the community and for revival to rise among the churches of our area.

Love Abbotsford was one of the first events on June 16, 2001. About 1,500 people from 30-40 churches in the city got together "to love the people of Abbotsford into a relationship with Jesus Christ by facilitating practical, intentional outreach." The purpose was to organize, orchestrate and surprise businesses and people on the streets with random acts of kindness. To love on people, beautify parks, hand out hotdogs, popcorn and bottled water on street corners, clean gas station bathrooms, rake the yards of the elderly, fix cars for single moms, bring a meal to a shut-in, garden, and just about anything you could think of that might bless someone randomly. We ended the day at Sevenoaks Church with storytelling videos of what God accomplished through His beautiful people of Abbotsford. The gathering also united us in a worship concert led by some of the worship leaders from various city churches. The celebration that evening involved story, video, interpretive dance, drama, and music. The worship music was recorded live and produced into a worship CD called *Love Abbotsford.* It was a call to a lifestyle of putting others before ourselves. Under the leadership of friend Kevin Boese, hundreds lived our theme verse: "And let us consider how we may spur one another on toward love and good deeds. Let us not give up meeting together, as some are in the habit of doing, but let us encourage one another—and all the more as you see the Day approaching." (Hebrews 10:24-25)

Interestingly, years later I heard of a town (Spencer, Iowa) near our current residence that had used the *Love Abbotsford* model and website to glean ideas to replicate the same kind of random-act-of-kindness day in Spencer. They had t-shirts made just as we had done which is why I observed and inquired as to what *Love Spencer* was when I saw a lady at Wal-Mart wearing a *Love Spencer* t-shirt. What a shock to find out that the Spencer event was modeled after something we had done way up in British Columbia years before! It kind of blew me away! I expressed great delight and surprise as we talked about our love for our towns!

After the *Love Abbotsford* event, other worship and prayer events were planned. As many as 66 churches in the city came together in addition to a few churches beyond our city's limits. Brian Doerksen and his band powerfully participated. The very first such event was held the evening of September 9, 2001 in Rotary Stadium. That was two days before the terrorist attacks of Tuesday morning, 9-11-01 in New York City. We will never forget either day. September 9 was a truly gorgeous Sunday with the setting sun shining on the mountains in the background of Rotary Stadium! Just breath-taking beauty! I have memorable photos of that night. Northview Church gathered for their fall kick-off at the stadium that morning, and they offered the use of their staging and equipment for the evening session. We arrived early for prayer and preparation. We prayed that someone—anyone—would show up. Rick and I confessed a bit of distress not knowing if anyone was interested in revival, prayer and unified Christian worship.

The article just two days later published in a city newspaper on September 11 (yes, 9-11-01) under the title *Spiritual revival: Thousands worship* accompanied by photos, stated, "An estimated 8,000 Christians prayed for the people in the City of Abbotsford and enthusiastically sang in worship at Rotary Stadium on Sunday night—easily the largest Christian assembly ever held in Abbotsford...Pastor Rick Porter coordinated the massive Christian unity event called 'Together—The Church of Abbotsford'...Porter noted that a miraculous spirit of unity and love is moving in this city and many young adults and teens are responding to the contemporary spiritual revival."

The article went on to name Brian among other musicians who led and created the "upbeat spiritual mood for the evening." *Canadian Christianity* magazine estimated 8,000 to 10,000 in attendance! What a sight! What a night! God was there in it all and He inhabited our worship! It was a spiritual goose bumps kind of night! Each church participating had paraded bearing colorful banners with their church name on them, affirming unity and participation across all denominations. It was a beautiful sight and sound!

Psalm 60:4 speaks of banners or flags on poles that were raised by those who loved the Lord as rallying points for troops in preparation for battle and for leading people into action. Banners were raised or lifted high in other Old Testament passages as well. It seemed fitting that each church created a large banner on a pole to parade through the audience that night. We desired to summon God, experience revival and a unified community in our region. That sight was memorable!

BC Christian News reported, "It was the night that Abbotsford Christians declared, to the city and to the heavens, their unity in the Lord, before an estimated 8,000 to 10,000 people...Pastor Rick Porter of Sevenoaks Alliance Church, chair of the event, called together all pastors and Christian leaders in attendance to kneel in front of the stage to demonstrate their commitment to unity. Many wept as Rev. Trevor Walters of St. Matthew's Anglican Church prayed a prayer of repentance and commitment. As he prayed, the rest of the crowd spontaneously rose to their feet to support the leaders."

The article continues, "There's something stirring in Abbotsford, British Columbia. A **birthing** some are calling it. Like woman with child, the church in Abbotsford is pregnant with a work of God's conception," says Porter, who also chairs the Abbotsford Christian Leader's Network (ACLN). "The clearest symptom is of coming together of churches. Though the work of unity God is doing in his church is not specific to Abbotsford, it has happened so quickly and so completely as to convince leaders that Abbotsford has an important place in a move of God that seems now to be virtually upon us," says Porter.

But there wasn't always such a corporate spirit, the article continued. "Abbotsford was not a happy experience for us," says Justin Rees of Upstream Christian Initiative. He was commenting on local reception to his ministry's five-year cross-Canada reconciliation tour, 1995-1999. "We didn't see any signs of enthusiasm for churches working together."

"Six years ago, for people to even think of going to a meeting in someone else's church was odd," echoes Pam Dyck, an acknowledged intercessory leader in Abbotsford. "Now it's like this is one big house of God and all the churches are just different rooms in that house; the doors aren't locked anymore."

Rick goes on to explain how things changed for all churches to cooperate, what were the pivotal events, and how Abbotsford was invited to stage the General Assembly of the World Evangelical Fellowship back in May 1997. Abbotsfordian Reg Reimer, a lifelong missionary and agent for global religious liberty took the lead. "It was too big for any one church to plan, so they had to work together," says Steve Klassen, then working with the Mennonite Brethren Missions Services International.

I personally was privileged to be able to participate in this exciting World Evangelism Fellowship event by playing piano at some of the sessions. Christian leaders from all over the world of every "tribe and nation" converged in Abbotsford. An unforgettable experience for Rick and me! A little touch of what heaven might be!

Working together to bring this event to our area seemed like a divine initiative. As Henry Blackaby describes in his book, *Experiencing God*, "Humans join God in what He is about to do." A passion of Rick's has always been to search out or find what God is doing and then to join Him in it. Bringing unity and cooperation to the body of Christ has always been a desire close to Rick's heart. It remains to this day.

That night after the city-wide event Rick was so afflicted by the enemy that he could hardly walk to the car when it was over. Brian knew that the enemy often attacks after great spiritual victories and he prayed diligently over Rick the moment the event was over. Praise God for spiritually intuitive prayer warriors who understand the battle!

Less than two days after the event, Rick continued to experience the most physically painful days. On September 11, Rick felt totally spent, chewed up and spit out and in the most excruciating pain of his life which we still don't fully understand. He was literally crawling on all fours. A professor from Trinity Western University who attended our church, came over to our house that morning because she somehow knew in her sensitive spirit that affliction and spiritual warfare might be attacking Rick's body and spirit. She offered her condolences on the events of that early morning attack on the World Trade Center (I could not sleep and happened to be up early and watched it on TV in horror as it all unfolded) and this lady prayed warfare prayers over us. She prayed powerfully for Rick and me and for the enemies of our soul to flee in Jesus' name.

After the events of 9-11, we transplanted Americans felt especially alone. Suddenly the powerful worship event from two days previous appeared to diminish in impact, lost as the lifetime deposit of 9-11 replaced, at least in our minds, what God had done. Maybe not in reality, but we were discouraged.

Yet Rick persevered and Rotary Stadium's miracle precipitated other events he led with the city coming together. Another event was called *Together Again*, held the first week of November, 2001. The photo and article in the newspaper said the event would run each evening for six days at Tradex, a convention center at the Abbotsford Airport. In these evenings, what occurred was simply prayer, music and worship led by area pastors and musicians. The gatherings were celebrative and celebrated with a cumulative attendance of approximately 15,000. The sessions grew each night.

A national event, the Canadian Prayer Assembly held May 4, 2002 was even moved from Toronto to Abbotsford's Tradex Convention Center because of the revival our city had been experiencing. Rick joined the national prayer leader, Brian Warren, to quickly organize and pull it together. Those days were continued visits from God and we have video of those amazing nights of the Canadian National Prayer Assembly. But Rick and I were afflicted in our physical bodies like crazy, particularly one night of the event. Oh, my! We have stories! It seemed opposed spiritually, but city intercessors walked the aisles and the circumference of the convention hall, surrounding and bathing it all in warfare prayers. There was an amazing breakthrough at the end of that time. It occurred when one young leader, led of God, acted out an outpouring of the Spirit on Canada by pouring oil on a Canadian flag and map. Individuals representing the languages and peoples of Canada knelt together to pray. The intense atmosphere of spiritual battle in the place broke, and freedom released in a sense of victory. Immediately, Brian Doerksen and his team took the stage and led in the only true moments of spiritual freedom that night. It had been a battle, but there was breakthrough. Greater is He who is in us than he who is in the world. Nothing could stop Rick from doing what God called him to do. Only God knows the ramifications of Kingdom work done in those days.

CHAPTER 6

Pit Time

I waited patiently for the Lord; He turned to me and heard my cry. He lifted me out of the slimy pit, out of the mud and mire; He set my feet on a rock and gave me a firm place to stand. He put a new song in my mouth, a hymn of praise to our God. Many will see and fear and put their trust in the Lord.

—Psalm 40:1-3

The first mention in the Bible of Joseph's pit is Genesis 37:23-25. In the *Holman Christian Standard Bible* we read: "When Joseph came to his brothers, they stripped off his robe, the robe of many colors that he had on. Then they took him and threw him into the pit. The pit was empty; there was no water in it. Then they sat down to eat a meal." The audacity of sitting down to a feast while likely regaling one another with stories of poor Joseph's predicament as the brothers shared a feast is stunning. All the while, they disregarded the screams and pleas of Joseph in the pit! Abandoned!

Job also refers to a pit numerous times in his great loss and suffering. He felt drawn to an early grave himself. Yet I knew that after Job's season of severe testing, God came with double recovery, restoration and recompense for all that Job had suffered and lost. (Job 42:10)

Now after all of the great victories, but also our sudden dismissal, we found ourselves doing pit time. I didn't sign up for it. As pastor and friend David Johnson warned, "Eventually, pain gets stamped on your passport." The Nehemiah wall-building was thwarted and actually seemed to secede, the favor of building community withdrawn. Laying down our trowels would be devastating to us. However we would still clutch our swords. God could have chosen to deliver us instantaneously from the pit (after all, we didn't deserve being thrown into it, but God gets to choose when we get out). In my reading and research, God often does not deliver out of the pit instantly. Slovenly spirituality can result when good things are happening, when our lives are on track and God seems to be abundantly blessing. A pit time is needed to change us and ultimately bless us. OK, how long, O Lord?

Get Out of the Pit by Beth Moore has some good thoughts on this. The pit is a real place we live in and we found in time that it was really hard to get out. It was a slimy, muddy place as it indicates in Psalm 40:2 where you "sink deep in the mud and mire." Jeremiah 38:6 describes the pit as a place of sinking down. It is hard to stand inside the pit. When we cannot stand, we are vulnerable to the real enemy of our soul, Satan. David cried out, "I sink in deep mire, where there is no standing." (Psalm 69:2, *NKJV*) It is a place where the trials in the pit make us ineffective and powerless. It's very difficult to stand up to offenses and assaults when we are knee deep in mud.

Beth Moore studied the Hebrew reference to the pit and came to the conclusion that "a pit is an early grave that Satan digs for us in hopes he can bury us alive. Should you fall into it, he really cannot make you stay." I learned also that God won't make me get out either. We cannot be passive in the pit. Ephesians 6:11 implores us "Take your stand against the devils' schemes." Stand your ground. "He set my feet upon a *rock* and gave me a firm place to stand." (Psalm 40:2b)

Psalm 94:18, 19 and 22: "When I said, 'My foot is slipping,' your unfailing love O Lord supported me. When anxiety was great within me, your consolation brought joy to my soul. The Lord has become my fortress and my God, the *rock* in whom I take refuge."

Beth goes on to talk about how dark the pit is—we sometimes cannot see things that originally were obvious to us. When we are in the pit we are convinced there is no place to go. Our eyes have adjusted to the darkness of the pit. "In a pit where vision is lost and dreams are foolish." How tragic. I love what Edith Edman said, "Don't doubt in the dark what God shows you to be true in the light." Satan is effective in making us question and doubt that God has our best in mind when we find ourselves in the dark pit. He knows God has the power alone for us to be restored and reconciled outside the pit. God is ultimately responsible for our way out in His time.

In spite of the struggles we face in our pit, these struggles do not refute or contradict the promises of a loving God. When we have had an extended stay in the pit we can affirm, "You intended to harm me, but God intended it for our good to accomplish what is now being done, the saving of many lives." (Genesis 50:20) He takes my pit time, my past pain and ashes and uses it every day as I yield to Him. The secret is Christ in me, not me in a deep pit of circumstances.

The story doesn't end in the pit for Joseph. Of course God had a plan all along to send Joseph on ahead to pave the way and make sure there was a remnant in the land, to save lives in an amazing act of deliverance. "So you see it wasn't you (the brothers) who sent me here, but God. He set me in place as a father to Pharaoh, put me in charge of his personal affairs, and made me ruler of all Egypt." (Genesis 45: 8) God would unfold our own personal plan for getting out of the pit. It wasn't fun at the time, but our story now from the outside of the pit is pretty incredible, as you will see. Our goals for recovery looked more like simple survival than did Joseph's rise to become a ruler of all Egypt. But we knew there was a good plan to unfold on our journey.

How did Joseph get out of the pit? How can I get out of my pit? Would it be a human deliverer or God himself? As you recall Joseph's brothers eventually removed him from the pit for the purpose of easing their consciences. They sold him for twenty pieces of silver to a caravan of Midianite merchants passing by. Genesis 37:27-28 tells the story. Joseph's ten older brothers lied to their dad about what happened. What Joseph endured after that may have been more brutal than had he just let the pit become his grave. I was pretty sure the way out of our pit would not be the result of getting sold to a caravan of traders! Yet it would take years for Joseph to realize a true Deliverer, and perhaps that would be true for us as well.

Human deliverers will fail us just like Joseph's brothers. They compounded the offense of abandonment by selling Joseph into slavery. He had to find his path through this humbling experience while waiting for the true Deliverer who is in it for the long haul. It doesn't necessarily happen on our schedule but He finally sets our feet on the rock as Psalm 40 in *The Message* affirms. There, David said that he "waited and waited and waited for God. At last He looked; finally He listened. He lifted me out of the ditch (pit), pulled me from deep mud. He stood me on a solid rock to make sure I wouldn't slip. He taught me how to sing the latest God-song, a praise-song to our God. More and more people are seeing this: they enter the mystery, abandoning themselves to God."

The Sovereign Lord alone is my strong Deliverer. Psalm 140:7 and 8, *MSG*, speaks of *crying out* to the Lord for mercy. "Listen to me! God, my Lord, Strong Savior, protect me when the fighting breaks out! Don't let the wicked have their way, God, don't give them an inch!"

Sometimes we have good support from friends, family and others who can help us in our pit time. Prayers and encouragement, advice and counsel can give us some hope. Our counselor, Dr. Radford, gave us professional counsel, prayer support and hope every time we drove in to Vancouver to his home. You may find some healing in that kind of support as well with someone who understands your plight and story. Helpers who come alongside a pit-dweller can sometimes be emotionally drained as they seek to help. It is easy for them to give up after a time. Then we may feel abandoned again. That was not our experience. Dr. Radford was wonderful and so helpful.

Divine rescue comes *at your wits' end* as in Psalm 107:27…and *in the nick of time* (verse 28). I have to repeat Psalm 107:25-32 from *The Message* —it is that good. "With a word He called up the wind—an ocean storm, towering waves! (Or a pit, if you prefer.) You shot high in the sky, then the bottom dropped out; your hearts were stuck in your throats. You were spun like a top, you reeled like a drunk, you didn't know which end was up. Then you called out to God in your desperate condition; He got you out in the nick of time. He quieted the wind down to a whisper, put a muzzle on all the big waves. And you were so glad when the storm died down, and He led you safely back to harbor. So thank God for His marvelous love, for His miracle mercy to the children He loves. Lift high your praises when the people assemble, shout Hallelujah when the elders meet!"

We learn that God waits for us to *cry out* to Him for help so we know from where the help comes and where the credit is due. As we confess our pride and sin we can sing the song of *My Deliverer*! It is just like God to bring me reminders of who my Deliverer is. Get this! As I was reading and contemplating this *very* sentence, an old Rich Mullins' song started playing on my old Kindle Fire via TuneIn radio. I just "happened" to be listening. I heard the melody (no lyrics) of the old tune. It was uncanny! I immediately had to Google the song for the precise lyrics in which, interestingly, the *captives* "call out" over and over: "My Deliverer is coming—My Deliverer is standing by." That is repeated many times. The lyrics go on to talk about the desert place, Jesus hearing the whole world *cry out* for healing and rescue that would flow from His own scars. He will never break His promise—He has written it upon the sky. How cool is that—for *everyone* to see the Deliverer? You can't miss the promise if it is written across the entire sky! He will never break His promise. "My Deliverer is coming—My Deliverer is standing by."

Hard things happen and our memory seems to fade. Our faith is enlarged as we remember Biblical stories of those who were delivered in the past. We can borrow from history as a metaphor for our own story and a template for hope in the present and in the future. We can invite God to save and deliver us now just as He did in the past. We can remember the deeds of the Lord as David did. (Psalm 77:11)

David did his pit time too. His pit was more a cave. His story begins in I Samuel chapter 19 as he is anointed King. He had slain his giant. He was a court musician, a leader in the army and was on his way to the palace.

By verse 18 David had fled to Rahma. By chapter 22 he escaped to the Cave of Adulum where he spent the next ten years of his life. With all supports, expectations and scaffolding of his life gone, David lost his job, his popular position and security, his wife, his dignity and self-respect. Yet in the middle of his cave time, God was his refuge and strength—help in the time of trouble.

For all you pit or cave dwellers, God understands about your cave because He's been there. Jesus was crucified and put into a cave of death. Yet I'm smiling right now because we know the end of the story—He arose out of that cave, transcending sin and death. "By His great mercy we have been born anew to a living hope through the resurrection of Jesus Christ from the dead." (I Peter 1:3, *NASB*) The resurrection of Jesus is a testimony to the resurrection of us pit-dwellers. All part of His plan!

God wants us to clearly comprehend and recognize that He is our Deliverer, eager to remove us from our pit. He has not lost track of me. I now hear this older song, *My Deliverer,* in a whole new light, once it comes time for a pit-deliverance! He is continually reminding us over and over that He is there for us...He's coming...He's standing by to be our Deliverer as we call out to Him!

Then as we *consent* (as Beth Moore puts it) to be removed from the pit, God draws close to us and does the extraction according to His good mercy. "Praise the Lord, my soul; all my inmost being, praise His holy name. Praise the Lord, my soul, and forget not all His benefits—who forgives all your sins and heals all your diseases, who redeems your life *from the pit* and crowns you with *love and compassion*, who satisfies your desires with good things so that your youth is renewed like the eagle's." (Psalm 103:1-5, emphases mine) Notice that after a pit extraction, love and compassion are outcomes for others who need our help. He doesn't waste our pit time. Many around me need the kind of help I can give them because of my pit time. We are struck down but not destroyed. When our foot has slipped we can say with the Psalmist in chapter 94:18-19 from the *New American Standard Bible*: "If I should say, 'My foot has slipped,' Your lovingkindness, O Lord, will hold me up. When my anxious thoughts multiply within me,

Your consolations delight my soul." I'm so glad that faith is the vision of the heart that sees God in the dark. Continue to hope in Him.

Sometimes we blame God for pit time because we cannot understand His ways. Just remain with Him long enough to discover the answer to any nagging questions you hang on to. The judge of all earth will do right. This takes me back to my first chapter on *God did this...*or at least He allowed it for a reason. He knows us inside and out and loves us so much He wants to make everything right. (Psalm 103:14)

For the record, even as we did our pit time, we were always nurtured and sustained. There were delightful seasons. "There is a river, the streams thereof shall make glad the city of our God." (Psalm 45:4) Spurgeon said, "A little stay on earth will make heaven more heavenly. All is well!" The pit stay on earth makes heaven more appealing.

We did not know what our next step would be. We cannot take shortcuts out of the cave. Uncertainty of the duration of pit-time struck fear in my heart. I understood God doesn't always reveal the future to us. The unknown made me shudder with looming possibilities. Yet, I was always assured that the Lord would hold and refuge us through it and would certainly bring us to a new place in our relationship with God. I did not need to strike out on my own. Faith and waiting would be the process. As I waited, there would be the "cake of bread," provision for each day.

God does some of His best work in the pit. That's where all you have is God—your help in time of trouble.

CHAPTER 7

Promise of Provision

Each day, though it bring its trouble, shall bring its help; and though you should live to outnumber the years of Methuselah, and though your needs should be as many as the sands of the seashore, yet shall God's grace and mercy last through all your necessities, and you shall never know a real lack.

—CHARLES SPURGEON

THE ABOVE WORDS of Spurgeon stood out as if in neon lights exactly when I needed them. After all of the wonderful stories during the Nehemiah building years in Canada, we found ourselves in confusing times of defeat and failure. We no longer had a "voice" in the city. Months went by and we felt more and more like Joseph in the pit. How long would we have to do pit-time? No job or income? I began to feel victimized and wallowed in self-pity.

Chuck Swindoll said: "Self-pity will lie to you. It will exaggerate. It will drive you to tears. It will cultivate a victim mentality in your head. We open the door to that when we establish an unrealistic standard we can't live up to. We need to allow God to set the standard. He is always loving, affirming, accepting, and faithful to uphold us. Self-pity is the smog that pollutes and obscures the light of the Son. The more you're in it, the deeper it hurts." Yes, we needed the light of the Son to shine into our souls.

I was surprised how painful and difficult it was. Why was God so silent—no clarity for our future? "Asking God for clarity may indicate an underdeveloped ability to fully trust Him." (Brennan Manning in *Ruthless Trust*) Ouch! That hurt! Possibly our faith and trust needed to be tested longer in order for it to be found reliable.

Noah didn't have much clarity when God told him to build the ark either. He had faith—no outward sign that a flood was coming. Not even a cloud in the sky. When the Lord commanded him to gather materials, build the ark to specifications, round up the animals and his family, he was mocked. He didn't really understand what the future would bring. No clarity...and then he waited and waited. He didn't create maps and charts for the journey; he didn't steer. Noah didn't try to figure out where in the world he would be going. God would bring clarity in time.

I had sung all my life: "All I have needed His hand hath provided." And another hymn, "Leave to thy God to order and provide...in everything He faithful will remain." I wasn't necessarily recognizing all the help I had anticipated for each day. Every day had its needs and the needs didn't always equal the provision. The needs came so regularly. I undoubtedly hurt the heart of God wondering where the "enough" was or questioning the timing of needed provision. It didn't always seem satisfying. Where was the evidence of His love and faithfulness? If I had seen it, it might have been easier to trust Him for the next day's provision and supply.

Something I ran across in a little old devotional book helped me to expect daily provision and not be surprised by it even though initially I felt the jar of flour and the cruse of oil seemed to be failing me.

I Kings 17 tells of Elijah asking the Widow at Zarephath to make him a small cake of bread from what little she had in her home, and also to make one for herself and her son. This request came after Elijah's long trek through the desert from Brook Cherith which left him extremely hungry and thirsty. Elijah assured her that provision would not fail. Verse 15 says that she did as Elijah had asked. "So there was food every day for Elijah and for the woman and her family... in keeping of the word of the Lord spoken by Elijah." Could I experience the same provision?

Charles H. Spurgeon spoke directly to my heart. "You, Rick and Dianne Porter (I added our names), have daily necessities, and because they come so frequently, you are apt to fear that the barrel of meal will one day be empty, and the cruse of oil will fail you. Rest assured that, according to the Word of God, this shall not be the case. Each day, though it bring its trouble, shall bring its help; and though you should live to outnumber the years of Methuselah, and though your needs should be as many as the sands of the seashore, yet shall God's grace and mercy last through *all* your necessities, and you shall never know a real lack." (*Daily Help* by Charles Spurgeon, Grosset and Dunlap Publishers) God was in the business of providing just what we needed, when we needed it—every day. I confess that I sometimes saw a world of lack, scarcity and injustice. Was God not wholly good? Can we perceive a God who supplies our necessities as needed rather than identify a mindset of scarcity?

Luke 11:2-4 in *The Message* says, "Father, reveal who you are. Set the world right. Keep us alive with three square meals. Keep us forgiven with you and forgiving others. Keep us safe from ourselves and the Devil." Yes, give us each day our daily bread. We wait for it. I would come to know His provision for daily supply and I don't have to be afraid that daily provision will run out. There is the promise of perpetual manna. God's provision!

CHAPTER 8

The Shattering Blow

God changes caterpillars into butterflies, sand into pearls, and coal into diamonds using time and pressure. He's working on you too.

—Rick Warren

There are seasons in life of suffering, loss and sorrow. Many are reversible; some are not. It puts a halt to business as usual. I am reminded again that there can be no fragrance without the crushing of the flowers, no wine without pressing the grapes, no oil without squeezing the olives and no real joy without sorrow. The squeezing, pressing and crushing didn't feel good! Some seasons of change might even require that we lose one thing before we can gain something else. OK, Lord! Waiting! Waiting for olives to be crushed to make the best oils, grapes to be squeezed to make the finest wines, roses to be pressed to make the most fragrant perfumes.

One of the amazing gifts of God that has come our way in the decade after we limped away from Sevenoaks Church is the joy of residing within one hour of our daughters and their families. The pain then was so dark that the joy of our more recent years could not be imagined.

In a visit to do some projects in the home in which my youngest daughter and family now reside, something caught my eye on the kitchen counter. To my surprise, I saw two large glistening geode rocks. That summer we had taken a trip to the Black Hills of South Dakota together, staying in a beautiful home (a retreat home for pastors) south of Custer, South Dakota. What a fun family time! Our grandsons wanted to dig for geodes at a place called Cosmos Mystery area. These geodes had been "planted" there so kids could have the experience of finding a geode, for a price of course. I Googled "geode" so I could learn how it is formed. As I read I understood it to be another metaphor for what God does in our lives.

The outside of the geode looks like a plain, normal rock. These round masses of mineral are hollow, formed by water or chemical precipitation. I discovered on *Wikipedia* that they are generally formed by the process of gas bubbles in volcanic rocks from minerals deposited from fluid or groundwater. Geodes commonly have crystal-like mineral quartz inside the cavity. Most contain clear sparkly crystals while others can occasionally have purple amethyst crystals.

As the boys eagerly found their geodes, the proprietors then used a big machine to crack the rock open to display the sparkling, glittering crystals inside. What wonder the boys then experienced! Something rough and drab, appearing decayed on the outside, revealed something beautiful inside. The surprise and secret was within the core of the geode. Sunlight would especially make them sparkle.

For the exposure of the shimmering crystals, the geode first had to be struck with a shattering blow. An awful impact was required to reveal the hidden beauty. The blow was not only an end, but a beginning. As Beverly LaHaye suggests in her book *A Different Kind of Strength*, "this shattering is the end of something ordinary...and the beginning of something quite extraordinary. Before the blow is struck, only the outside of a nondescript, ordinary-looking rock is visible to the human eye. Afterwards when the broken pieces of the rock are exposed to the light, we marvel at the intricate beauty of its glittering, crystal formations that were hidden deep at its center." She continues, "Some blows of life merely shatter a small hope or dream. Others are totally devastating and seem to leave life broken beyond all repair."

We need to focus on the gem and the beauty revealed on the inside after the shattering blow. God can make something beautiful in our inner empty place...with time and space and something to water and expose it.

It may seem tragic to us and feel like it comes with a high price. Ultimately, true magnificence can be revealed with the blow. Sunlight and Sonlight make it shimmer more brightly.

Beverly LaHaye also tells of tempered steel being forged into sterling quality. Tempered steel goes through a process that gives it the capacity to retain its shape, flexibility and cutting edge despite hard usage. Realizing the potential for the steel depends upon the right circumstances. "Nothing short of being put through the fire and being hammered again and again will produce the finest tempered steel. So it is with fortitude. This sterling quality of character can only be forged through long periods of struggle and patient waiting."

"God needs a chisel tool to do His transforming work. The tool God uses most often is adversity, difficulty, hard times, irritations, struggles, opposition and suffering. Suffering produces perseverance; perseverance, character, and character, hope. Adversity strips us down, exposes us, and breaks us—all prerequisites for genuine spiritual growth. Suffering makes us aware of our need, our weakness and our sinfulness. It drives us to God. In our adversity, God becomes present and active." (Jerry Sittser in *When God Doesn't Answer Your Prayer*, page 161)

As I contemplated other jewels that are a product of pain, I remembered the precious oyster and its tiny pearls "conceived through irritation, born in adversity, nursed by adjustment." Chuck Swindoll writes of this in his book *Growing Strong in the Seasons of Life*. For some reason, the shell of the oyster gets pierced by a tiny grain of sand. Without wounding and irritating interruption, no pearl could have evolved. The pearl is a symbol of stress, is covered and the wound is healed into a gem. Irritation must finish the work to mature and complete the beautiful pearl. I knew what needed to happen.

CHAPTER 9

A Quiet Place

Come with me by yourselves to a quiet place and get some rest.

—Mark 6:31

One day we received a phone call from someone in Arizona who identified herself, but I did not know her. Today, caller ID may have prevented me from answering the call. I am grateful it didn't! She explained that a relative of hers attended our (former) church. God had called her and her husband to devote a second home in the Okanagan area of British Columbia as a retreat place for pastors as a gift and blessing. She invited us to get away to this quiet place for as long as we needed. What a blessing from an angel stranger!

We were more than elated to accept their offer. The house was fully furnished and the shelves were stocked with some food staples. A library of books and music CDs were available for our use. What breath-taking beauty around this Okanagan Valley home! The landscape of our own home in isolation had become bland. So, we packed up and traveled toward solitude, calling on God for direction and teaching at the school of Jesus' feet, for resting, restoring, whatever God might grant us. The view was incredible! Slow, quiet walks and drives through the area around the big lake and prolific fruit orchards known in that area were exactly what we needed. Vineyards were everywhere. Maybe our deep hurt would fade as we drove this unparalleled landscape defined by the Basin of Okanagan Lake. The painted fields of wild yellow-headed flowers that resembled daisies were infused with God's glory!

I wanted to spend some time reading in this quiet place; I desperately desired help and insight. It wasn't until this time that I could actually focus on anything like reading an entire book. In fact I was struggling with losing some of my memory, which I learned later is a symptom of a deep hurt or loss. Another deeply hurt pastor's wife took me to "school" regarding loss of memory. It was good to know that I was not alone and not too crazy. My mind had been in such a state of confusion.

Sleepless nights became a collision, a whip-lash of sorts, of soul and mind, in attempting to unwrap the tangled thoughts and feelings. Because of one of my medical conditions, I was wearing a Holter monitor to record my intensifying tachycardia (racing heartbeat) which I had experienced to some degree for more than 25 years. This only seemed to occupy more of my focus at the retreat home. An episode of a few years previous was not forgotten. I survived an emergency room visit for atrial fibrillation with a heartbeat of more than 240 beats per minute. The "doom and gloom" drug, as the cardiologist called it, adenosine, was administered via IV but had no effect after two doses. I was almost given the paddles to shock my heart back to normal rhythm. Intravenous meds continued over many hours to slow the heartbeat, yet the rhythm was still not back to normal when I left the hospital.

While resting at the home in the Okanagan, I recall pushing the recording activator because my heart would race until it was hard to breathe. I was spent. God must be teaching me something through this, I thought. In spite of anxiety and a racing heart, I tried to focus on learning what God was saying through any book, any song, or any leisurely walk. I had been quoting for months from II Chronicles 12:27, "We do not know what to do, but our eyes are upon You." That didn't seem to be getting me anywhere!

The first book I picked up from the retreat home library was an old, worn little paperback book called *NEVER, NEVER GIVE UP* by Jack Hartman. I was drawn to it for some reason because it appeared so old and worn. That must be a sign of a good book, tried and true! The first thing I read was, "God doesn't want us to hurry." Oh, my! Hadn't we already waited long enough? "Our Father never hurries. He is always at peace." I had so much to learn from this little book. Pages of notes resulted. I learned that I needed to be calm and continue to wait patiently for God.

No place in God's Word instructs us to hurry. "Our Father has perfect rhythm. He causes the tides of the ocean to come and go on a precise schedule. The moon keeps track of the seasons. God sets the times. We must not get ahead of Him." It encouraged me to meditate, study the Word, pray, worship, yield control to the Holy Spirit and trust God one day at a time. "Sufficient for each day is its own trouble." (Matthew 6:34b, *AMP*)

If we cross bridges before we come to them, we waste emotional energy. If we worry about the future, we dilute our effectiveness in the present (Luke 11:3). He provides daily bread—just what we need for today. Psalm 104:14-32 in *The Message* tells how beautifully God orders everything in creation. At His fingertips He controls the entire earth. We need to take one day at a time, wait and trust Him.

I learned from another book: "Men often call their petitions unanswered because in their impatience, they do not give God time. If we give God time, He usually does something bigger and better than what we could have imagined, making even fairy tales seem trite and boring." (Harry Emerson Fosdick) This was a truth and promise that was fulfilled in time in our story.

Jerry Sittser, writing in *When God Doesn't Answer Your Prayer*, says, "God's redemptive work requires a great deal of time and space. What God is up to extends far beyond what the eye can see and the mind can imagine. We cannot be in a hurry, as God has His own sense of timing which is usually slow..." At that time, the process seemed like an eternity!

I journaled this prayer after taking many helpful notes, "Dear Father, I don't have the strength or ability to keep going in the face of my problems. I will be still; I will be quiet and calm down because I *know* you are God. I'm certain you will take care of everything that concerns us during this time and send us a job as we trust in you and wait on you. My world seems to be in total turmoil, yet I know you are in complete control. The battle is not ours, but yours." (II Chronicles 20:15)

While you wait, never fear that God is not at work. Isaiah 64:4 in the *New King James* confirms, "Since the beginning of the world men have not heard nor perceived by the ear, nor has the eye seen any God besides You, who acts for the one who waits for Him." He is always up to something big that our eyes and ears can hardly comprehend.

The Okanagan retreat house offered quiet CDs. The music washed over me. One song that seemed to keep coming up everywhere we went was "...you give and take away, blessed be your name." God can place what He wants in your hands or take out what He desires. Yet, blessed be His name! I will praise Him in the storm.

While at the retreat home we attended a little church in Winfield, British Columbia. On that Sunday, the message was just exactly for Rick and me. And they sang (He gives and takes away) *Blessed Be Your Name* by Matt Redman. God's song for us followed us everywhere!

As I quieted myself to listen, I learned that I could not realize or attain God by necessarily adding anything to my life or in my soul, but I could grasp and recognize God by a process of subtraction right now. What are the things God desires that I subtract from my life in order to know Him more deeply? Blessed be His name even when He takes away. What if less is really more? Were there things in my life that were adding, subtracting, multiplying or dividing my calling? By subtracting stress, disobedience and rubbish, I could add value to my life. It was gratifying to be with God alone and enjoy it. Adding the upright/noble/blameless and subtracting the evil/corrupt/depraved.

The promise of "arrival" and "rest" is still there for God's people. God Himself is at rest. And at the end of the journey we'll surely rest with God. "Okanagans" do come to us. At other times, we trust and rest to make all days Okanagan days wherever we are. "So let's keep at it and eventually arrive at the place of rest, not drop out through some sort of disobedience." (Hebrews 4:11, *MSG*)

CHAPTER 10

Resurrection Hope

Where there's life, there's hope…Oh! May the God of green hope fill you up with joy, fill you up with peace, so that your believing lives, filled with the life-giving energy of the Holy Spirit, will brim over with hope!

—*Romans 5:13, MSG*

Every sunrise gives us one more day to hope. His mercies are new every morning! As long as there is hope, joyful living can happen. We have the hope that "there are far, far better things ahead than any we left behind." (C.S. Lewis)

While we were in the Okanagan area on our resting retreat, the gift from the Arizona couple, we decided to take a drive along beautiful Okanagan Lake near Kelowna, British Columbia. We passed through an area that had been destroyed by a bad forest fire in the late fall of 2003. We were amazed at the devastation and loss of any vegetative life in that once green forest. That fire storm burned for an entire month. Over 240 homes were lost. Viewing this devastation resonated with me. Burned up and lifeless! I took lots of photos of miles and miles of nothing but blackened tree stumps.

We drove down the road toward a little hill upon which stood a few buildings that were completely untouched by the fire though everything around them had been destroyed. As we got closer the reality of the miracle began to sink in. We realized it was a Catholic retreat center in the middle of what used to be a beautiful landscape. We could not imagine how those buildings had been preserved in the fire. I thought it only HAD to be God! There was a miraculous story in there somewhere.

I asked Rick if we could stop to go in and talk to someone about it and how the miracle happened. It seemed in my heart that it could somehow parallel our journey and I wanted to know this story. Rick was reluctant so he stayed in the car while I went in. After hunting around to find someone, I did hear their story. Wow! God had specifically answered the prayer of those that administered the retreat center. The campus was miraculously spared in the fire as a result of their cries for help and preservation during that wild fire. A metaphor of what God could do for us! Isaiah 43:2: "When you pass through the waters, I will be with you; and when you pass through the rivers, they will not sweep over you. When you walk through the fire, you will not be burned; the flames will not set you ablaze."

In November of 2004, over a year after that first devastating fire, I learned that the mountains of Kelowna in the Okanagan area of British Columbia were again blazing. This time the fire fighters were doing many "controlled burns" up on the mountain tops to remove charred, lifeless trees and debris. With controlled burns the environment would be readied to bring forth new growth and life. People in the area were concerned because the fires looked "out of control."

Kathi Pelton, in an apparent intimation from God as she watched these later fires burn, blogged, "Encourage My people. The fires in your lives and in the lives of the corporate body are 'controlled burns'. These fires are under my watchful eye and I am in control. I am burning away the debris from the fire storms that have come upon you. I am clearing the land of your life both individually and corporately for new life to come forth. Do not be afraid. Allow them to burn away. Keep your eyes fixed on Me and do not panic or fear that these fires are out of control even though they appear to be. I am controlling these burns. They are necessary for what I am about to birth and bring forth...Allow the old things (old nature) to be burned away so that the new can come forth." Wow! Another confirming word for us! I was so excited to come across this prophetic word by God's grace. He is good!

A short time later a sweet couple from our former church sent us a card. On the front of the card was a photo they had taken labeled "The Resurrection Tree." It was a large-headed hydrangea-like tree in the midst of blackened earth. The photo was dominated by a burned tree with charred lifelessness all around it. But ah, how amazingly beautiful were the large white blossoms, now blooming again, contrasting to the blackened tree and earth around it! The white blooms on this tree were the only appearance of life in the entire area. Life, beautiful life, bursting forth again out of the devastation. One single resurrection tree in the middle of that burned landscape! That would become another metaphor of our resurrection hope! To this day, I enjoy studying every detail of that photo. It touches me deeply. Thanks Ron and Kathy for the life-giving image.

What a wonderful gift the retreat home was to us at just the right time! Lots of lessons learned!

Upon our return home to Abbotsford from the Okanagan, we discovered someone had anonymously placed an envelope in our newspaper box next to our front door. It held a worship CD and cash. I speculated who it was from because he misspelled my name on the envelope which I had previously known him to do! God's provision! He wrote that this was the beginning of "seed" provision for the days ahead.

A couple from church invited us to go yachting with them for several days near Desolation Sound in the island waters between Vancouver Island and the Canadian mainland. What a gift! Two bedrooms, kitchen, living room seating area, decks on both ends—TV, reading material, you name it! God granted us serendipities, sparkling jewels of His grace, and He shouted to us in those days on the ocean. Desolation Sound was part of our healing from the sounds of desolation that had haunted us.

One day a large pod of dolphins swam with our yacht, a very specific performance as they played and dove all around our boat. Just for us! Hundreds! They would speedily get ahead of us and then fall back to swim with the boat! Beautiful synchronicity! It was a gift and smile from God! I have videos that I treasure of the frolicking dolphins and of our time on the ocean. I believe those hundreds of dolphins were sent just from God for us! I am so glad we got a video of it!

Finding waterfalls was a delight. We anchored and hiked up from the ocean to hidden areas where we found streams cascading into the ocean. What refreshment for our souls. Creation calls us to God! How can anyone not see it? Great graces from God!

One evening we anchored for the night in a cove. As we sat at dusk into darkness after dinner (which we usually enjoyed on the back deck), we saw the most amazing lights I'd ever seen called phosphorescence. It is a luminous appearance of a dancing, bouncing light show of sparkling jewels on the waterscape. I learned on the internet that this happens at certain water temperatures, producing iridescence from slow oxidation of phosphorus after exposure to light. These organisms leave eerie blue-white trails that dart and dance on the water. I had only heard of such a phenomenon. I was mesmerized. How this would be captured in my memory! I never imagined viewing this in my lifetime, being a Midwesterner. Desolation again failed to live down to its name.

Setting traps for our evening crab meal was fascinating and the traps were filled as needed. Even a little octopus and star fish caught in the trap surprised us. Walking on the beach for special shells was a delight. This was not the only time we were blessed by this couple's yachting invitation.

God also used an epiphany moment during an earlier yachting time to speak something specific and clearly to Rick that he had been asking God about for some time. Something of huge significance! It would take too long to tell the story but it was God shouting to him from the yacht as to what to do going forward. I'll just say it had something to do with the compass and the plates on which we ate our meals—designed compass plates! The answer was right there! Rick followed God's obvious direction, a specific answer to his questioning heart, through the metaphor of many compasses we were watching. Amazing how God can speak specifically into a situation if we have ears to hear and eyes to see God. He is in the details! Thanks Ingrid and Murray for your gift to us.

A man stopped at our door late on Sunday, November 7, 2004. It was getting dark outside and his coat and hat covered much of the little I could see of him. I didn't immediately recognize him in the dark as a man from our former church. We were so alone at that time that it was unusual for anyone to come to our door. He handed me an envelope and said God had told him and his wife to do something for us and his note said, "Please accept this gift as from the Lord." He turned and walked away. Inside was a check for $1,000! The note attached is still in my possession. God's provision! God promises to provide during our pit time. It granted us new hope and trust in God for His amazing provision and renewed hope in God's people, not all of whom abandoned us. Thanks Bert and Julie!

I was still very sick and because steroids were prescribed, I couldn't sleep much at night, my breathing was labored, my ear thumped loudly and incessantly. At that time it seemed like I had taken steps backward. My little mustard seed faith was presented to God and I continued to trust Him, in spite of how awful I felt, for healing, leading and direction.

A pastor from another church in town asked if he and his elders could come over to pray with us. Their visit was a gift! We all gathered in a circle in our living room and they prayed for provision, healing and direction for us and for God to hold us close to His heart during that time. One elder prayed and spoke a word over me that I would dance again. "Dancing again" had been a metaphor for me. Others had prayed that over me as well. I had written a month or two earlier in my journal from Tim Hansel's *You Gotta Keep Dancin'*, "God can blow the lid off any box, unfold it and turn it into a dance floor." And I added, "I will freely pirouette in my spirit again." God was saying to me, "Don't permit your situation to make you feel boxed in. I will turn it into a dance floor." After prayer time and words of hope, this pastor and the elders handed us a check for $1,500. Later at Christmas they gave us an additional $1,500! God's provision! Bills were being miraculously paid! Other church leaders in our town cared about us and became part of our blessing.

All of these gifts were an assurance of resurrection hope. I've seen an acrostic for HOPE—Hold On, Pain Ends. Then I found another one—Have Only Positive Expectations. A bit cheesy, but they work for me.

"The Lord is good to those whose hope is in Him, to the one who seeks Him; it is good to wait quietly for the salvation of the Lord." (Lamentations 3:25-26) Our hope was rising! We could enjoy God's great graces in the midst of our tough time. As we drank deeply of the graces of God's promises, He made us stronger through everyday circumstances. We could boast in our weaknesses so that Christ's power would rest on us. Uncovering our soul to let grace and hope soak into our core!

Hope was our confidence that things were going to get better. Because decay and death are always around us, earthy hope is fragile at best. Heavenly hope is a vision of redemption in the midst of the decay and disappointments.

CHAPTER 11

Less Like Scars

People will learn more from your scars than your trophies.

—*Caleb Grimm*

My daughter Nikki, knowing I enjoy music and was in need of some encouragement, compiled a CD called *Mourning into Dancing*. The second song on the CD was Sara Groves' *Less Like Scars* which I valued and played over and over:

Less Like Scars

It's been a hard year
But I'm climbing out of the rubble
These lessons are hard
Healing changes are subtle
But every day it's

Less like tearing, more like building
Less like captive, more like willing
Less like breakdown, more like surrender
Less like haunting, more like remember

And I feel you here
And you're picking up the pieces

Forever faithful
It seemed out of my hands, a bad situation
But you are able
And in your hands the pain and hurt
Look less like scars and more like
Character

Less like a prison, more like my room
It's less like a casket, more like a womb
Less like dying, more like transcending
Less like fear, less like an ending

And I feel you here
And you're picking up the pieces
Forever faithful
It seemed out of my hands, a bad situation
But you are able
And in your hands the pain and hurt
Look less like scars
Just a little while ago
I couldn't feel the power or the hope
I couldn't cope, I couldn't feel a thing
Just a little while back
I was desperate, broken, laid out, hoping
You would come

And I need you
And I want you here
And I feel you

And I know you're here
And you're picking up the pieces
Forever faithful

It seemed out of my hands, a bad, bad situation
But you are able

And in your hands the pain and hurt
Look less like scars (x3)
And more like Character
(Used with permission—saragroves.com)

Nikki also made a video for us with that very song in the background some time later, but that story will come in proper sequence. We were not finished with "scars" yet, as you will read. Sara Groves' music and lyrics would become among my favorites. Later I was privileged to meet her in person as she ministered at the Okoboji Bible Conference where we now serve.

Scars show us where we've been. That we've been hurt. They do not dictate where we are going. Jesus bears scars in His hands for us. How can we forget His great love for us? He tells us that none of our scars can make Him love us less. He did everything that needed to be done when He said, "It is finished." (John 19:30) My scars indicate that You, God, will never abandon me. Have you ever pondered why Jesus kept the scars in His resurrected body after His crucifixion? It is the one identifiable effect of His death that could be touched and seen. He chose to keep them. It was a permanent reminder of His suffering for us. His wounds and scars are His calling card. His power has not been diluted since that first Resurrection Day.

I recently saw a picture of many shelves, full from floor to ceiling, of leather boots. It was an interesting photo of various kinds, colors and sizes of very old, worn boots with lots of creases, dings and scars. The sentiment over the picture was "where the leather is scarred, there is a great story to tell. What stories do your boots have to tell?" (blackmtn-ranch.com) Each scar I have makes me who I am over time. They never completely go away, but neither do they hurt any longer, as Philip Yancey wrote in a devotional. Scars are evidence of healing.

We are often afraid to ask someone how they got their scars. We look away in embarrassment, sometimes in fear of knowing or sometimes out of sympathy. It is just too hard to engage the story of the scar. Yet, anyone with scars has a story to tell, and to that point, they have survived. We never have to be ashamed of a scar, a battle wound. It simply means you were stronger than whatever tried to hurt you. It is a constant reminder of the hurt, the memory, but also that "the hurt is over. The wound is closed and healed, done with." (Harry Crews, *Scar Lover*)

Scars indicate survivorship. Trophies indicate participation. Your scars help make you who you are. They are not a place where pain is still being harbored; they are a sign of healing that has been brought out of pain. Scars tell of something preceding but do not define our future. Scars bring back ugly reminders in our lives but also make us realize the beauty that has been created through them. The beauty of our scars is something to celebrate. When we acknowledge the beauty in our brokenness God is honored.

My daughter who gave me the *Less Like Scars* CD, now long after her CD gift, displays her own cancer scar, wearing it as a strong warrior. She is still in her process of "survivorship" and "participation." We are trusting and walking through this journey with Nicole in all confidence that God's got her covered in this, and her character is emerging beautifully.

CeCe Winans album, *Throne Room*, washed over me as I came to the Throne Room to worship. I worshipped my way through pain and scarring, listening to God's voice of truth. As I worshipped, worry seemed to vanish. Worry cannot add a single hour to my life anyway. (Matthew 6:27) I'd intentionally worship! I'd intentionally praise and thank Him because He is worthy. Offering thanks helped me release control and acknowledge God's strength and care for us. We give thanks not just for the pleasant things, but the scars, the hurt, and in all situations. It helps us to grow in our capacity to see God's love and power at work in all the details of our lives. When praising, God draws near to us, we overcome the enemy, our perspective is changed, and it can be an antidote to depression.

Any praise to God thwarts Satan. He hates any praise not directed toward him. We need to use this weapon more in our lives. It reminds

Satan that God is still Sovereign and supreme in spite of all his evil efforts to discourage. To make praise even more authoritative and powerful towards God and against the enemy, couple it with God's Word, and especially the truths that magnify Jesus as the Victor. Psalm 149:6 from the *New American Standard Bible* relates to our spiritual warfare as we can rejoice in God's triumph over the enemy: "Let the high praises of God be in our mouth, and a two-edged sword in our hand." Music was one of my ways to "worship with eternity in it" as A. W. Tozer put it.

God revealed so many truths during the quiet time of isolation. The Good Shepherd was carrying this lamb close to His heart. He feels what we feel because He became a Lamb too. I began to hear the Good Shepherd's heart beat again as I'd climb up into His lap to get close to His heart and His care.

Jesus was tested at every point as we are. He understands not just the fact of our situation but also the feeling of our infirmities. I needed to remember what God had done through us in the past and to thank Him. Remembering God's perpetual care is a theme of Deuteronomy. As Moses prepared Israel to enter the Promised Land, He reminded the people of all the ways God took care of them for 40 years. Moses knew that recalling God's past mercies would give the Israelites strength and hope for the future.

A. M. Gurnall likens it to a hound on a hunt. "When a hound has lost the scent, he hunts backward to recover it and pursues his game with a louder cry of confidence than before...Look backward to see what God has done for you..." This was a reminder of His perpetual care in the past that helped me to pursue with a louder cry of confidence. Phillip Yancey said it memorably, "I have learned that faith means trusting in advance what will only make sense in reverse."

Yet, I don't know why this was all so hard. Some asserted that their pain was much greater than our pain. Others implied that any mature Christian should be able to handle this as God's Sovereign best and in His mercy...and, get over it! It is true; countless friends were stumbling through life with much greater pain than we could ever imagine. Harder things than we were experiencing. Pain cannot be compared. Yet knowing that did not make our pain any easier.

As Corrie ten Boom said, "Hold everything in your hands lightly, otherwise it hurts when God pries your fingers open." Did our knuckles need to be pried open?

We can spend an entire lifetime dwelling on our scars and what we've been through or we can proudly carry them as a reminder that we have lived and they are a symbol of the wounds that God is healing or has healed.

My niece Tara Porter Livesay, a missionary in Haiti, posted a powerful message on Facebook. She agreed that the quote to follow is not easy to hear. There is no doubt that real living and deep loving will leave us bruised. But the alternative is so much worse. "So go out and live real good and I promise you'll get beat up real bad. But, in a little while after you're dead, you'll be rotted away anyway. It's not gonna matter if you have a few scars. It will matter if you didn't live." (Rich Mullins, in concert in Lufkin, Texas in 1997)

CHAPTER 12

The Pulpit Again

I was unsure of how to go about this—I was scared to death, if you want the truth of it—And so nothing I said (or preached) could have impressed you or anyone else. But the Message came through anyway. God's Spirit and God's power did it, which made it clear that your life of faith is a response to God's power, not to some fancy mental or emotional footwork by me or anyone else.

—I Corinthians 2:4, MSG

Six churches in our town and region contacted us and asked us if we would permit our names to stand as candidates for open pastorates. We knew in our hearts that would not be the best plan since we believed that some friends possibly would follow us to another church within the community. As much as we were hurt we did not want to hurt the local church we loved by "stealing sheep" nor did we want anyone to follow us. So we waited…and waited.

Rick was invited to preach as a guest in various churches. It took six months after not preaching to begin to accept such opportunities. Rick lost his confidence and especially in proclaiming God's truth in front of Christians. Self-doubt and super sensitivity paralyzes potential and he felt he could only give to others if he had a proper, healthy opinion of himself. He felt he didn't have much left over to give to others. He was also afraid of his own wounded anger. Would he manage it well or would it pour out in the pulpit in an unhealthy way? He was scarred and scared.

Satan can use a nagging sense of inadequacy to isolate one and destroy our dreams and our giftings. "If people can't see what God is doing, they stumble all over themselves; but when they attend to what He reveals, they are most blessed." (Proverbs 29:18, *MSG*) The fear of failure again has a way out—never getting back into anything risky. It can be immobilizing, cause us to shut down and do nothing. Yet Paul even spoke of many wise and noble supermen and superwomen who were not chosen to fulfill God's purposes. (I Corinthians 1:26-31) It was in the weaker ones, through their feebleness and flaws, in which God showed His power. God does not use superstars to do His work—from Moses who stuttered to Mark who ran out on Paul and Barnabas. God uses people with infirmities and flaws and gives them work to do, and then supplies them with sufficient grace to do it. They show God's marvelous power through weakness. We cannot boast in a calling, in successes, in education, or in a gifting. God delights in our weaknesses, in insults, in hardships, in persecutions, in difficulties. Paul boasts in irony: "And so the weaker I get, the stronger I become." (II Corinthians 12:10, *MSG*) I also love verses 7-9, "Satan's angel did his best to get me down; what he in fact did was push me to my knees. No danger then of walking around high and mighty! At first I didn't think of it as a gift, and begged God to remove it. Three times I did that, and then he told me, 'My grace is enough; it's all you need. My strength comes into its own in your weakness.'"

"One reason Satan continues as the accuser is because his job is easy when we doubt ourselves. (See Revelation 12:10) He knows that even when we're innocent of any reason for being in the pit, we are well aware that we are far from innocent in other things. He plays mind games with our consciences so that for the life of us, we can't seem to distinguish between those areas where we are guilty and those where we are innocent...Satan is the master of using our own insecurity against us. He knows that deep in our hearts we are so fragile and injured by sin and life that his faintest whisper will talk us into feeling guilty even if we may not be. Satan knows the hardest person to forgive will always be one's self." (Beth Moore in *Get Out of That Pit*)

It was hard to overcome the struggle of haunting self-doubt, the disappointments that seemed to drown possibility. These weapons are from Satan to bring defeat and feeling of failure and wasted gifts. They destroy dreams. It is false theology that it brings holiness or sanctification. Not so! Matthew 5:43-48 straightens out the order. When you love God and yourself and others, you are fulfilling the whole law of God.

Remember Numbers 13 and 14? God had a vision for His people. A beautiful dream of the Promised Land. Moses sent the cream-of-the-crop military into the land of Canaan to check out the land which flowed with fruit, grapes, pomegranates, milk and honey. (Numbers 13:23) Yet what the reconnaissance party described was the incredible strength of the giants in the land, the cities appearing as forts. They described themselves as grasshoppers compared to the sight of the descendants of Anak (verses 31-33). The envoys began to weep and were scared to death. Only Caleb and Joshua had different perceptions. David Seamands clarifies, "Their observations were the same but because their perceptions were different, the conclusions were different as well. As a result God's great dream for His people to be delivered from slavery in Egypt was detoured and delayed for forty years! All because the people were not ready, due to their low self-esteem."

In spite of not quite feeling ready, the first opportunity for Rick to preach that he accepted was one I remember well. It was in Vancouver. The encouraging part of guest preaching was that many of our friends from our former church drove to Vancouver to hear Rick preach. In my journal, I listed all those who came to support and love on us. It was comforting and the large delegation blew us away with their encouraging presence. Rick also preached in Oliver, British Columbia and a few other churches. His confidence began to increase.

"This priceless treasure we hold, so to speak, in a common earthenware jar—to show that the splendid power of it belongs to God and not to us. We are handicapped on all sides, but we are never frustrated; we are puzzled, but never in despair. We are persecuted, but we never have to stand it alone: we may be knocked down but we are never knocked out." (II Corinthians 4:7-9, *Phillips*) Rick would preach in weakness through handicaps with God's promised strength and anointing.

I guess nothing builds self-confidence like just getting out there and doing the thing you fear the most and again feeling God's smile, refusing Satan's accusations and defeat. Andrea Bocelli admits to not having an extraordinary degree of self-confidence, but he knows the gift he has been given is from God. He shares that amazing singing gift with as many people as possible and does not permit his weaknesses to derail his passion.

Rick gradually and humbly began to move in his giftings again. He did not need to try to impress anyone (his coat was already stripped of him). The truth spoke for itself as God's Spirit became clear. Joshua 1:9 has presented truth throughout Rick's life, popping up in the most appropriate moments. "Have I not commanded you? Be strong and courageous. Do not be frightened, and do not be dismayed, for the Lord your God is with you wherever you go."

CHAPTER 13

Signs and Wonderful People

Some people come into our life as blessings; others come into our life as lessons.

—*Mother Teresa*

Along our journey we counted too many blessings and lessons to be ungrateful. We were bombarded with God's reminder of his provision through people—strangers and friends. Lessons from God on the path of our journey were too obvious to not enumerate and exclaim, "God, you are so good!"

God was giving me eyes to see His care in the details of everyday life, in *my* circumstances. "Everywhere we look there are traces of God—in history, in our circumstances, in every nook of humanity and every crannied flower of creation. If we look with the right eyes, listen with the right ears, we will understand the natural creation as a form of sign language through which God expresses Himself." (Ken Gire in *Windows of the Soul*)

From Aurora Leigh

Earth's crammed with heaven
And every common bush afire with God;
But only he who sees takes off his shoes.
The rest sit around it and pluck blackberries.
—Elizabeth Barrett Browning

Strive always to remember that you are in the immediate presence of God, and strive to act as you would if you saw the Savior standing by your side—or even carrying you. Then take off your shoes and see the common bush afire and alive with God. Unfortunately, most of the world is asleep. "Only a few people are fully awake, and they live in a state of constant total amazement." (from the movie, *Joe Versus the Volcano*)

"Blessed are those who see beautiful things in humble places where other people see nothing." (Camille Pisarro) Desiring those traces of God and burning bushes, and having eyes to see them, helped me understand that God was working in my life continually. We need to see and listen, actively wrapping our senses around the moments He gives us and then to enter those moments. People who desperately want the Presence and glory of God get it because God is looking for those people who He can support.

Journaling was invaluable because I could look back to see His goodness even in the simple moments. God's goodness was growing from the common bush into the tall redwood tree. The world is studded with wonders and there are ribbons of God's Presence woven everywhere if we have the eyes to see them.

In today's world we all seem to be in perpetual motion. It's too easy for life to be filled with distractions, activity, and obligations rather than the places of holy ground where every common bush is afire with God. In those times I recalled the goose bumps that had faded on my arms and in my memory. The goose bumps would return reminding me that my heart was still intact. Those moments were sacred with dreams of enlarging the strong place where I stood in the journey. A place where our dreams could become reality again.

Photos and art spoke to my heart of God's goodness. My brain is wired that way. I can cry just looking at a picture and discern what God is saying to me through it.

Michelangelo's painting on the ceiling of the Sistine Chapel was a "wow" to me. How much God loved me! Someone had sent a greeting card to me with this work of art on it. We have all seen Michelangelo's portrayal of the finger of God reaching His hand down to connect with Adam's finger, but their fingers almost, but not quite, touching. So close, though. It symbolizes God's relationship to all mankind in all of human history. Whenever He reaches us, a window opens between heaven and earth in a moment of revelation—words of God's grace, love, guidance, correction, wisdom, understanding, forgiveness, assurance. Words for which our soul hungers and longs. Do you feel abandoned by God—a gulf between God's finger and yours? He's reaching out to you. Open your eyes to His presence in your weakness. Reach up. He will never abandon you. (Hebrews 13:5)

This art along with the *Pieta*, also by Michelangelo, would bring tears of gratefulness and joy as I would dwell on the passion in the painting. A message delivered by Karen Mains at the Okoboji Bible Conference some years back had awakened to me the passion in this painting as she focused her message on the *Pieta*. For some reason I cried through most of that message as I contemplated the deep love of Jesus, the Sacrificial Lamb, and the love of his mother Mary holding Him, bearing Him with compassion in her arms.

Another famous painting by Anders Zorn features a couple dancing in a ballroom. It makes me smile. This art was the cover of a wedding invitation we had received. I had tucked the picture in my journal as a reminder of the dance. It was my "dance again" picture and hope-filled metaphor. Many had prayed specifically that I would indeed dance again.

A framed print of this very art called *The Waltz* now hangs on my living room wall as a reminder of the dance! A friend, Cheryl Wells, unexpectedly presented it to me soon after we moved to Iowa. I was blown away and asked her how in the world she was aware of my dance metaphor and the very same artist's rendering of *my* dance? It was the very art on the wedding invitation we had received years before. Cheryl understood "the dance!"

We shared our own stories as we shared the dance. The kindred heart memories still warm and amaze me. She told me she had thought of me when she saw this very dance print hanging in the Biltmore in North Carolina. She had to search for a framed copy of the painting for some time before she found it.

She presented it to me at Okoboji Bible Conference one day immediately after the speaker, Pastor Dave Johnson (lead pastor at Church of the Open Door, Minneapolis), had spoken on "the dance" on that very Sunday morning, August 7, 2005. No coincidence! Cheryl already had the framed art ready to present to me in the trunk of her car that day before hearing this message on the dance. Isn't that just like God?!

I was absolutely blown away by the miraculous convergence of God's Spirit in us and the timing of this gift and its theme—and the theme of the speaker that very same day. I have listened to that message again, via CD, and have been blessed all over again.

David Johnson's message was on the dancing heart of David from II Samuel chapter 6. He danced before the Lord at the beginning of his reign as King in celebration of the return of the Ark of the Covenant to the centrality of God's people. It is what he for so long desired. The ark represented and was symbolic of God's promises, power, presence, provision and covenants. The story behind the dance revealed David's heart, the pure jubilant joy.

With every dance there is a picture or a story! David Johnson spoke of his own family moments of his dances of celebration in his life. He said you might dance for a desire or for the fruition of a dream. King David danced because the glory of the Lord had departed (I Samuel 4:21) and had been gone for so long when the ark had been taken away—God's presence. Then the ark returned. David actively desired that God would consume him and his people with the manifest Presence of God. What most of us want are the "goodies" or what spins off of the Presence—like peace, healing, comfort, Easy Street, or whatever you want to label it.

David Johnson went on to talk about the church at Sardis that had the appearance of being alive, but they were dead. They were still a church but the glory of the Lord had departed. Some despaired of that and others didn't even notice because the church seemed to be well-crafted and, by all appearances from the outside, operating and functioning effectively. He cautioned against that attitude or mentality. We desperately need to desire the glory and presence of the Lord. We need to be people of the Presence. Those people who want it, get it. Otherwise, how can we be distinguished from the world? I was ready to dance!

Cheryl's art gift of "The Waltz" was a reminder God was doing something in my heart as He revealed His presence, and we have become kindred dance friends. I remember each time I look at "the dance" on the wall of my living room! I deeply desired the dance again! It was happening!

While editing the manuscript for this book, I ran across a trailer for an upcoming 2015 movie called *Desert Dancer*. It certainly caught my attention. It is a true story of a young aspiring dancer in Iran who risked his life for his dream to become a dancer despite a nationwide ban on dancing. His dance company went underground and even to the desert to dance in seclusion amidst Iran's politically volatile climate. I saw a clip of the small group dancing in the middle of the desert and it touched my soul. Even amidst political repression or the dark night of the soul, we can dance freely if the passion and dream is there with the hope that wells up within me! There's another painting for someone—dancing in the desert!

There was another "aha" moment which would later become extraordinarily significant! A couple who occasionally attended our church, whom I had never met, invited us over for dinner one evening. This was some months after our removal from Sevenoaks as we still traversed our own desert of isolation. She was the sister of the then Executive Director of Bethel Seminary in Saint Paul, Minnesota. Rick had graduated from Bethel Seminary and knew her brother. That evening we enjoyed lamb with mint jelly for dinner and as the conversation continued, Georgette, with big tears in her eyes said with deep conviction, "I believe God MUST take Rick out of Canada to save his LIFE." What in the world did that mean? Rick and I didn't know what to think of that statement and were puzzled why she said it, filled with such deep emotion, through tears. We thought the assertive comment was a bit strange and we promptly dismissed her declaration for years. But the word would prove prophetic.

Another couple invited us to breakfast one morning. Though they were from our church, we did not know them well. They told us how much our ministry had meant to them and their family over the years. Their lives had been radically changed! The stories warmed and salved our weary souls. Their words were incredibly affirming as they shared of God's grace upon their lives as a family! They pulled out a check for $1,000 for us to use as needed! It took our breath away. I still have a myriad of emails from them through the years of how God grew them spiritually in miraculous ways while we served the church family. God's provision! In isolation time, God ALWAYS provides! Over and above all we could ask or think. They invited us for delicious meals to their home. Thanks, Denver and Jorlean and family! We are friends to this day! You have touched our hearts.

A couple from a church in Minnesota where we had served in our younger years committed $100 every month to us. Their monthly gift was like perpetual manna. God's people provided and filled us with holy astonishment. Thanks Carol and Fred—Fred now in heaven.

I continued to have health issues and infections. I was prescribed steroids for severe rhinitis and a bad cough. One day I chose a new clinic with a female doctor I didn't know. I was pretty much a physical and emotional mess, even though I attempted to trust God for each day. This doctor was clinical and professional but after listening to my symptoms, asked me, "Is there something going on in your life right now to add to stress?" I burst into tears and the exam table shook with my heaving sobs. At that point in time, I had not cried that hard. I could not regain my composure to be able to talk. I wasn't sure I could divulge the truth anyway. We had been instructed by denominational leaders to keep quiet.

Before I launched into anything, I asked this physician if she attended a church in town because I didn't want to implicate our church in any negative confessions. She said she attended the very church from which we were asked to leave. OUR church? Seriously? Immediately she realized I was her pastor's wife and placed her hand on my back to calm and compose me. Her entire demeanor changed to one of deep empathy. And I sobbed louder. Our church was big enough that many attended whom I had never met. This physician was even a children's Sunday school teacher in our church. I did not ever remember seeing Dr. Campbell previously at church. She ministered deeply to me in every way and even declared at that moment that on behalf of anyone at the church who hurt me, to please forgive them. I'm crying now as I recall that serendipity from God to my soul when I needed it the most.

Dr. Campbell immediately proceeded to order the right tests for me, expedited and carefully followed up on everything in minute detail and care. This doctor was like an angel placed right where and when I needed her. God had kept her *from* me *for* me in that very moment. We kept in touch for a couple years after we moved away and I was able to let her know how much she had ministered the deep love of Jesus to me at the very time I felt so alone and needed it so desperately, along with the gift of her medical mercies and expertise. That moment of tears was a huge release for me.

At one of the lowest points in his life David reminds us of God's comfort and faithfulness. He wrote, "You have seen me tossing and turning through the night. You have collected all my tears and preserved them in your bottle! You have recorded every one in your book." (Psalm 56:8, *LB*) Or Psalm 42:3 in *The Message*: "I'm on a diet of tears—tears for breakfast, tears for supper. All day long people say continually to me, 'Where is thy God?'" As I pondered these words I found it amusing to wonder how many tear bottles in heaven bear my initials! He does record my lament. It can be freeing to let them flow and go, allowing Him to tenderly collect and preserve them. Where does he collect them? In his root cellar or fruit room? A wine cellar? A store room? As a gardener and preserver of vegetable and fruit produce, I envision this as comical. Labeled bottles of tears with the date of their preservation on the bottle or jar on the shelves! This demonstrates how much He cares about our grief. "So much is distilled in our tears…not the least of which is wisdom in living life. I have learned that if you follow your tears, you will find your heart. And if you find your heart, you will find what is dear to God. And if you find what is dear to God, you will find the answer to how you should live your life." (Ken Gire in *Windows of the Soul*)

Tears are therapeutic, a release, a cleansing. I tend to be embarrassed and wipe them away or just keep a stiff upper lip, but God collects and preserves them. He remembers them; He dries them. Just as this doctor cared for me with such grace and tender love until the day we moved away, I knew God tended us like a shepherd and gathered us lambs in His arms and carried us close to His heart (Isaiah 40:11). God's provision again! Thank you, Dr. Milena Campbell. May God continue to use your skills mightily to bring love, healing and peace to all for whom you care, as you administer the love of Jesus to those with all kinds of needs.

Those examination room tears came so suddenly, unexpectedly, and in waves of sobs from deep inside. It is interesting to think about it and what the tears may mean. "Whenever you find tears in your eyes, especially unexpected tears, it is well to pay the closest attention. They are not telling you something about the secret of who you are, but more often than not God is speaking to you through them of the mystery of where you have come from and is summoning you to where, if your soul is to be saved, you should go next." (Frederick Buechner from *Whistling in the Dark*)

Around the time of Christ, tear bottles were common in Egypt and Rome. As mourners approached the burial site for a loved one, they wailed loudly, collecting their tears. The more tears collected the more the deceased was loved. Women were sometimes paid to follow the mourners and weep into bottles. In so doing, the expression of love for the departed was enlarged.

Ken Gire's prayer for courage through releasing tears is:

> Help me, O God. Give me the courage to cry. Help me to understand that tears bring freshly watered colors arching across the soul, colors that wouldn't be there apart from the rain. Help me to see in the prism of my tears, something of the secret of who I am. Give me the courage not only to see what those tears are revealing but to follow where they are leading. And help me to see, somewhere over the rainbow, that where they are leading me is home.

Eventually my landscape of tears would turn into what I read in Isaiah 51:3: "I, God, will comfort my people, comfort all her mounds of ruins. I'll transform the dead ground into Eden, her moonscape into the garden of God, a place filled with exuberance and laughter, thankful voices and melodic songs." *(MSG)*

CHAPTER 14

Leaving Ruin

Circumstances may appear to wreck our lives and God's plans, but God is not helpless among the ruins.

—*Attributed to Eric Liddell, Olympian and Missionary*

THE RUINS WOULD one day be rebuilt. I would wait. God never intends to ruin or break us completely. His process is to reshape and design us. The longer He lingers over this process, the more we should realize we are exceedingly valued. Job 5:8 speaks of God wounding us, but He also binds us up. He injures, but His hands also heal.

On occasion friends would invite us to drive to Vancouver with them to take in amazing theatrical shows that were in abundance there—and I LOVED it! Our dear friends, Walter and Lori, hearing of a drama that might bless us, took us to Vancouver to see a live drama production of the book *Leaving Ruin*. It was the story of a pastor removed from his church, The First Church of Ruin, Texas, and what he and his family went through as they journeyed through that time of the unknown and how God was playing hide and seek with them. I tucked extra Kleenexes in my purse, knowing it would stir and salve my soul at the same time.

Before the play ever began, the pastor actor walked out on the totally pitch dark stage (we could not see him) and soulfully and mournfully, deliberately and slowly, began singing a cappella, "There is a Balm in Gilead…that heals…the soul..." Out came the tissues! How haunting and beautiful at the same time. Crying within seconds before the actual show began! I felt sorry for the young man sitting next to me, who probably was too young to have ever visited "ruin." He had no choice except to endure my tears and tissues. I blurted out some sort of apology to him for the torrent of liquid emotions.

Wow! I understood and lived that play. Through this pastor's confused but loving eyes, we saw the duality of divinity and humanity. I knew I must not be alone in the pit! That book/drama seemed to be just for me! David Biebel's book *If God is So Good, Why Do I Hurt So Bad* talks about the two faces of pain—human and divine. The human face is haggard, drawn, contorted and streaked with tears. The divine face is calm, assuring, kind and loving, but likewise, streaked with tears. Tears were OK.

City intercessors came to our home to pray for us. They emailed such encouraging words and Scripture verses and, to this day, I have kept a binder of the many emails that so ministered to our hurting souls. I just reread one of the many emails from intercessor Pam Dyck. As many had affirmed, she wrote, "You don't have to do this alone...There is a city full of leaders and people who LOVE (her emphasis) you and Rick!" Aww! She was always affirming and sent the most precise and timely words from God with Scriptures of confirmation. Agnes Doerksen, Brian's mom, was another dear soul who was burdened to intercede for us continually! Susan Anquist emailed one day that she had been awakened twice in the night to pray for us. What a gift of intercession! Korky Neufeld and Orlando Wall sometimes traveled to wherever Rick was speaking, even distances, just to intercede for him before and during his ministry. They amazed me with their prayerful loyalty. They stuck by us for the two years we remained in the city with no employment and even came to sit with us at our farewell. To this day, Pam, who grabs ahold of the throne, calling out to God, still prays for us and sends amazing words from God to our souls via email on occasion. Whenever I reread them, I am blessed all over again! What a gift! Our friends, the Unraus, still send us daily texts with Scriptural prayers and loving words.

Trips to the grocery store were almost excruciating for me. Invariably I would see people from our church who didn't understand what was going on or were curious why we were still in town after so long. Some of them would go out of their way to avoid me and to hide. I had leprosy! One woman would escape from a door not meant for the shoppers to exit. Seriously? Others would say awkward, thoughtless things when caught off guard, which only hurt more. Some, expressing great shock, thought we had moved away long ago to pastor another church of choice and were stunned to see me still in town. I avoided grocery stores at all costs. Rick rarely left our home to appear in any public shopping place. It was just too painful. He "did" isolation better than I did.

If you know of any discouraged, hurting people, think twice about what you say to them. They don't need any more guilt or insensitivity piled on top of distress and pain. They do not need critics. They hurt enough as it is. Please give them a word of encouragement and let them know you are an available safe sounding board. Or make a commitment to pray for them. And certainly don't begin to share your own woes which are "greater than yours." Yes, this did happen to me. Of course there are always more devastating, penetrating, painful situations than ones we often experience ourselves. I reiterate, I am fully aware that my problems are small potatoes. However, pain is pain and cannot be measured by intensity or degrees. And do not remind the one in pain that maturity in the faith means you should be able to handle it with effortless ease and peace, all the while singing "*Que Sera Sera*, whatever will be." And even though Romans 8:28 is true, I did not want to hear it just then. Nothing *felt* like it was working together for my good!

Yet, God's provision continued to flow in incredible ways as sparkling jewels of God's grace. I knew without a doubt that it was God. Sparkling jewels scattered in our dark pit places! Serendipities! Dancing phosphorescence! Rick calls each a "grace de Dieu." A street named Grace de Dieu, which we had walked in Paris, France, gave us this phrase. It means grace of God. We loved traveling Grace de Dieu!

I have dreamed of walking that street in Paris again someday, but perhaps every golden avenue in heaven will bear the name.

God's fingerprints are everywhere if we have eyes to see it. Rick reminded me repeatedly, "The physical (or natural) realm often shows us the spiritual realm." We live in the natural, but learning to live by the supernatural while existing in the natural is how we become people after God's own heart. Metaphors, given by God, are signs of His presence and blessing. Impossible to miss! I repeat, God speaks to us in dreams, art, stories, music, our wildernesses, our pit times, movies filled with grace and redemption, childhood memories, books, every day events. What a gift! Right before our eyes! Daily! God's provision! Impossible to not see!

My spiritual eyes began to see God and signs of His care all around me. He's in the details of life. He is working His plan. He is at work in the details even when life seems to be falling apart. It requires faith to learn to see the working of His hand. It requires courage to accept God's right to reveal Himself in the manner of His own choosing without us questioning His goodness or love for us. Ann Voskamp's book *One Thousand Gifts* affirms that God is in the details, in the moments. God is framed in the moments of our lives. Look around; see His fingerprints!

There is an eloquent prayer by Joshua Abraham Heschel which describes the richness of the ordinary:

> Dear Lord, grant me the grace of wonder. Surprise me, amaze me, awe me in every crevice of your universe. Delight me to see how your Christ plays in ten thousand places, lovely in limbs, lovely in eyes not his, to the Father through the features of men's faces. Each day enrapture me with your marvelous things without number. I do not ask to see the reason for it all; I ask only to share the wonder of it all.

Open my heart Lord to small daily wonders—each blessing you've shaped that blossoms and sings. Infuse me with your holiness in the light of your Presence.

CHAPTER 15

Cherries, More Cherries, Eagles and Grace de Dieu

The grace of God means something like: Here is your life. You might never have been, but you are because the party wouldn't have been complete without you. Here is the world. Beautiful and terrible things will happen. Don't be afraid. I am with you. Nothing can ever separate us… Like any other gift, the gift of grace can be yours only if you'll reach out and take it. Maybe being able to reach out and take it is a gift too.

—*Frederick Buechner in Wishful Thinking*

Grace is favor. Unmerited favor! Here is one of those favor fingerprints. This story was a huge gift from God for me. Our house in Canada was landscaped with a trellis of two varieties of Concord and Thompson grape vines and a plum tree in the back yard, an apple tree and two bing cherry trees in the front yard, along with fragrant flowers all around the house. There were roses, and gorgeous dahlias in the backyard. Between our house and our Guatemalan neighbors' house was a long row of hot pink rhododendrons in various shades. How I loved when everything was in bloom. Candy for my eyes! My grapes always produced plenty to eat fresh, enough to process canned juice and make lots of grape jelly every year. The same was true with the plum tree. Canned plums and jam! However, the apple and bing cherry trees seemed to grow taller and taller every year but just did not produce fruit. I wondered why the pollination had not worked to produce any cherries. The trees had been there for years. They were very tall...and barren.

Poof! Just the summer we needed grace, those cherry trees produced buckets and buckets of cherries for the first time. It was absurdly crazy and beyond description! As the Buechner quote at the beginning of this chapter says, we could reach up and take those gifts of grace—those cherries! Even the "reaching out" was a gift! There were so many cherries that I froze them in ice cream buckets to eat like popsicles. I canned them, made cherry pies and froze them to bake later, gave buckets of them away to neighbors and still had them coming out of my ears! The most beautiful huge cherries I had ever seen! The cherries were so productive that I call them my "cherries of joyous abandon." Truly a gift! That was a sign and metaphor to me again of God's provision for us just when we needed it. An overnight change from a barren to a lavish tree! I've used photos of those beautiful huge cherries to make greeting cards ever since. My resurrection *cherry* tree! A sign of abundant provision.

Sometime later as we packed to move away, I still had frozen cherries to give away to neighbor friends! God's amazing grace made me grin from ear to ear as I gave bag after bag away. I am still smiling about those cherry trees today and so grateful to God for that sign of provision. Again Rick's words came back to me—the physical realm shows us the spiritual realm. How amazing and true! God was working His plan and providing. Even through prolific cherry trees! A party complete with colossal cherries! Cherry pits heaped high! A grace of God! (I'm transiently daydreaming this moment of being in a pit, eating so many God-cherries and accumulating so many discarded pits that they eventually build up in piles for a foundation in the pit, allowing me to climb out of my pit! You know, like the fable of the farmer trying to bury the donkey in an abandoned well.) In any case the moral of the fable is true. Every adversity can be turned into a stepping stone toward freedom and hope.

I ran across a quote that I love from Martin Luther: "Even if I knew that tomorrow the world would go to pieces I would still plant my apple

(I can't help but read *cherry*) tree." That's where the blessing and provision was found for me.

Fast forward with me for a moment: About four years later after we had finally moved away to the States and we returned for the first time to Abbotsford for the funeral service of a pastor colleague and friend, we drove by our former home to revisit the place. I was curious. How would the house, yard and those productive cherry trees look four years later?

To my shock and horror, those cherry trees were gone—cut down. Removed! The front yard looked barren. Roses gone! I burst into tears. How could the new owners do that to my sparkling jewels from God? Why didn't they appreciate such productive trees? Something that vital, productive and meaningful to me? How could such a meaningful abundant grace of God become so useless to the new home owners? Why were these jewels of provision and grace cut down? I was surprised again by my torrent of tears. (You must think I cry all the time. I really don't! I just report each time I *do* cry)!

Upon our return home from the Canada funeral trip and reporting to praying friend Pam Dyck about the cut down cherry trees, she shot back an email suggesting that God's provision was just for us for that time. She suggested that the trees being gone were not a negative sign as much as a sign to Rick and me that their provision was for us and us alone. Not for the new home owners! Those that came after did not appreciate or see the provision they were initially there to bring. They cut them down because they were short-sighted, but at the same time, the provision of those trees, the abundance they brought in our last year there, was a supernatural sign for us only. It was not something God would do for the new owners or renters. "Supernatural provision is for the true Shepherd, not for the hireling," she continued. "I have the sense that even if the trees had remained, their abundance would have stopped—and perhaps already had—which would have resulted in their being cut down!" It made sense to me despite my frustration that they were gone. Pam felt it might also be a sign of *release* in the sense of our ministry there. We were absolved or freed of any expectations still floating around in our minds.

I began to understand more clearly God's unfolding plan even if it wasn't what I expected.

Somehow I had understood *release* the day we revisited our former house and viewed the barrenness of that space. This intercessor friend included other spiritual insights in the email that encouraged me and she suggested that God may be releasing us from the *burden of the call* that still felt unresolved in our sudden departure from our church. I'm thankful for prayerful friends who see God in our story too!

I reflected on Rick's weighty call of God again. What did the premature release mean? Let me repeat an earlier statement: "When deep desires (of God's call) and obstacles collide, the result is intense emotions, confusion, anger, frustration and pain." But release was a relief!

There were other metaphors, in addition to the harvest of cherries, which God granted us to keep us going during those lonely days in Canada. Eagles! We lived in a valley surrounded by snow-capped mountains and eagles were not at all a rare sighting. But God brought them right to us to soar over our car as we traveled. This happened frequently. A sign from God! And if God cares for the birds of the air, how much more He cares for us! Matthew 6:26: "Look at the birds of the air; they do not sow or reap or store away in barns, and yet your heavenly Father feeds them. Are you not much more valuable than they?" Soaring eagles were sparkling jewels and a winged grace de Dieu. We saw them everywhere we went and just expected it. And under those wings we were safely abiding. The common sight pointed us to God, and to keep looking up. We were expectant!

Our friends, Henry and Velma Braun, invited us to use their quiet Cultus Lake home any time. Cultus is a long winding lake tucked between the mountains. We had our own key. My brother even spent some time up there while writing one of his books. Gracious gifts to us! It was an occasional get-away and those times were refreshing, healing times as we would read, rest, listen to the still small voice, and relish in God's beautiful creation. *Creation Calls* (thank you, Brian Doerksen—YouTube it; you will be blessed by this music video).

One day I saw an injured seagull on the meandering footpath around Cultus Lake. I walked there often, listening for God's voice. The seagull was too injured to move, find sustenance, or fly away, but it spoke loudly to me in the silence. I bent over that paralyzed seagull which could only look at me with frightened eyes, and I suddenly felt like that seagull. Wounded wings. Too wounded to fly. Helpless and suffering. Tears streamed down my face as I told God I felt just like that helpless bird. How could I help the seagull? Someone HAD to help him lest he die on the rocks. If the truth be told, one of my sparkling jewel eagles probably failed at the prey (and lunch) of that seagull! God and I had a defining moment as I cried out my heart to Him bent over that dying seagull. I heard Him say back to me, "You *will* fly again. *Wait* to see what I will do! You will mount up with wings as eagles, run and not grow weary, walk and not faint." (Isaiah 40:31) And I found shelter beneath His wings. After lingering as long as I could, contemplating the parallels with my story, with difficulty I walked away from the dying seagull. Its eyes desperately crying for help without tears.

After time, a dear friend called to ask Rick if he would consider baptizing their three sons in Harrison Lake in British Columbia. It had been their favorite family lake for boating over the years. We had been to that beautiful area to see an international sand castle building contest on the huge Harrison Lake beach a few times. I had never seen anything like it in my life! Hot Springs in the area drew tourists from everywhere to the beauty of that place. This friend, Dorita, told Rick that the only pastor her boys knew in their growing up years was Pastor Rick. She asked if he would be gracious enough to travel to Harrison Lake with them for the baptisms. Rick had nothing better to do (a lot more fun than sitting around home... waiting...) and Rick said he'd be happy to grant their request. It would be a great delight!

They boated to a beautiful beach area and Rick conducted the baptisms. Upon finishing conversation and profuse thanks for granting the boys this blessing, they pulled out a card with a note and $1,500 check. Totally unexpected! God supplied AGAIN! Overwhelming grace and provision of God! I have read this over and over again and still am in awe of that moment of provision. It was blessing enough to be honored to baptize the boys—no remuneration needed! But it was God's faithfulness in abundance, and we continued to know He would always provide for us in our pit time. Thank you Smith family! Let the generations hear and rejoice!

CHAPTER 16

Still Still

At the still point, there the dance is.

—*T.S. Elliot from Four Quartets*

God was supplying every need in miraculous ways, but we were still sitting still and waiting on God to direct us to the next place. Joseph and pit time seemed to be way too prolonged. What are you doing, God? How long do I have to wait? The pit was making me claustrophobic and miserable. He reminded me, "Sit still, my daughter." (Ruth 3:8) Hadn't I already learned that?

Sitting still may mean we can never know what will happen tomorrow. God, in His Divine wisdom, has withheld that information from us for our own good. If we knew our future, would we not try to change our destiny? We would be overwhelmed by what we knew.

Stillness and quietness is not always easy in today's fast-paced life. But to be an imitator of God requires that we come to terms with the value of quietness, slowing down, coming apart from the noise and speed of today's pace of life. "Be still and know that I am God: I will be exalted among the nations, I will be exalted in the earth." (Psalm 46:10) Take a long look at your most High God by stepping out of the merry-go-round, whirlwind and traffic.

I love I Kings 19:11-13. Elijah experienced a supernatural engagement on Mount Horeb. He went to hide in a cave to try to bolster his shaken faith in God. Or maybe out of curiosity with the repeated desire of a moving of God that had been recorded there in the past. God had spoken there. But Elijah was also afraid of threats from Jezebel and was depressed that the people of Israel had abandoned God's covenant. God gave him bread before the journey to the Mount and warned that it would be a long and tiring journey.

God took Elijah out of the cave where he was sleeping for an experience God would unfold before his very eyes. God promised He would pass by. Elijah heard a hurricane wind and saw the terrible effects of it which caused an earthquake with rocks cascading everywhere. Verse 12 says, "But God wasn't to be found in the wind. After the wind, an earthquake, but God wasn't in the earthquake. And after the earthquake a fire; but God was not in the fire: and after the fire a *still small voice.*" A gentle, quiet whisper. The dramatic manifestation of the Divine glory could cause an earthquake and fire to erupt which prepared a highway for God to speak to Elijah in a still small voice. God did not speak to him out of the wind, earthquake or fire, but it surely got his humble attention and reverence. Yet God chose to make known His mind to him in gentle soft whispers. Elijah wrapped his face in his cloak as one afraid to look upon the glory of God. He did not cover his face throughout the earthquake and fire, but only when he heard the still small voice. Should we be more affected by the tender mercies of the Lord than by His terrors? I need to be still. I need to hear His still small voice. Step out of the rapid-paced life in order to practice being still to listen for His powerful whispers.

It causes me to think that with all the awful world events of the day in which we live whether God might need some dramatic way to get our attention so we can then give our reverent devotion and responsiveness to His still small voice. He reaches us sometimes most deeply and profoundly in a still small voice.

We need to accept God's right to reveal Himself in any way He chooses without us questioning His goodness or love for us. The work of God does not need to always be accompanied by dramatic manifestations or revelation. Divine silence does not necessarily mean divine inactivity either. It helps us grow in our capacity to see God's love and power at work in all of the details of our lives, whether they be dramatically great or pleasantly small. The Gospel is a gentle voice of grace, mercy and love.

Psalm 46:10: "Be still and know that I am God." Everything today calls us away from being quiet. Only a deliberate act can force us to stop to hear the invitation to come by ourselves to a quiet place. Being still before the Lord is an unnatural call. To stop moving for a time, to sit in attentiveness to His personhood and presence! It is a gift to Him and also to us. He offers peace to our souls if we sometimes modify or adjust what we are doing to engage the stillness. If we arrive in His presence on empty, having run from task to task, it will take discipline and time to wait for the fullness of God to come.

Hannah Whitehall Smith wrote in the book *A Christian's Secret to a Happy Life* that she would wait until she was happy in Him before she would leave her devotional time. Daily waiting brings us to that place of restful dwelling. We need to dwell and rest in a still, quiet place. How we neglect to incorporate this or plan for quietness in our lives. I am guilty!

Scripture regarding *waiting* kept on bombarding me and I knew it was God. "Be still and rest in the Lord; wait for Him and patiently lean yourself upon Him." (Psalm 37:7, *AMP*) Psalm 31:15 says, "My times are in your hands." "Let us not lose heart and grow weary and faint in acting nobly and doing right, for in due time and at the appointed season we shall reap, if we do not lose heart, loosen or relax our courage and faint." (Galatians 6:9, *AMP*)

My journal contains lists of "be still" Scriptures that I would review. I had no idea how many "wait" verses were included in the Bible as I studied them. The Scripture affirmed that I needed to not rush...sit still...in complete trust that God was indeed in control. In time I would see the deliverance of the Lord. "The Lord will fight for you; you need only to be still." (Exodus 14:13, 14) I needed to humble myself and also remember that this *is* temporary. God would take us through this one way or another as I submitted to Him. One day at a time.

I'd read somewhere that waiting itself might be necessary, creative and useful, like watching a forest gradually recover from a devastating fire until it becomes more beautiful than before. Yup, I've seen that! Just sit still...and...wait. Hard to do.

David even wondered if God was procrastinating or late in His promises. Psalm 31:1-5 from *The Message* reads, "I run to you, God; I run for dear life. Don't let me down! Take me seriously this time! Get down on my level and listen, and please—no procrastination! Your granite cave a hiding place, your high cliff aerie [sanctuary] a place of safety. You're my cave to hide in, my cliff to climb. Be my safe leader, be my true mountain guide. Free me from hidden traps; I want to hide in you. I've put my life in your hands. You won't drop me; you'll never let me down."

I realized that the Lord promised the captives in Babylon that they would return to their land in 70 years! Wow! And I couldn't wait a little while? God's good plans were not instant! God said to me, "No, not yet! I love you too much. But my grace is sufficient."

Lewis Smedes, in his book *Forgive and Forget*, talks about how difficult waiting is. "Waiting is our destiny. As creatures who cannot by themselves bring about what they hope for, we wait in the darkness for a flame we cannot light. We wait in fear for the happy ending that we cannot write. We wait for a 'not yet' that feels like a 'not ever.'"

He cannot be in a hurry; God has His own sense of timing. But He is never late. His timing doesn't conform to earthly timing (II Peter 3:8, 9; Psalm 90:4; Ecclesiastes 3:1). There is an end to this ordeal I'm facing. I would have to lean and learn trust in His timing. Psalm 37:7 and 9: "...Be still before the Lord and wait patiently for Him..." Psalm 37:34, *NASB*: "... Wait for the Lord and keep His ways. He will exalt you to inherit the land... you will see it." Philippians 4:11; Galatians 4:15; Galatians 6:9; I Timothy 6:8; Hebrews 13:5; I Thessalonians 5:16, 18; Psalm 87:7. Isaiah 64:4 in the *King James 2000 Bible says*: "Since the beginning of the world men have not heard nor perceived by the ear, nor has the eye seen any God besides You, who acts for the one who waits for Him." WAIT! "Stay with God! Take heart. Don't quit. I'll say it again: Stay with God." (Psalms 27:14, *MSG*) Psalms 130:5-7 in *The Message* rather shouts it: "Wait for what God will say and do. My life's on the line before God, my Lord, waiting and watching till morning...Wait and watch for God—with God's arrival comes love, with God's arrival comes generous redemption."

"Stay calm. Life is not an emergency. It is brief and fleeting, but it is not an emergency. Nothing that happens is unexpected with God. He's always in control...How long does it take for your soul to realize your life is full? The slower the living the greater the sense of fullness and satisfaction...Hurrying without entering fully the thing in front of me doesn't make up time, but throws it away. Hurrying makes us hurt, empties the soul and we miss the wonders..." (Ann Voskamp, *One Thousand Gifts*)

Habakkuk was given a vision by the Lord saying that the answer would be manifested or fulfilled at a specific time. It would not deceive or disappoint. "Though it tarry, wait earnestly for it, because it will surely come. It will not be behind on its appointed day." (Habakkuk 2:3, *AMP*) Habakkuk was wrestling and complaining to God. He was perplexed that wickedness, oppression and conflict were rampant in Judah. Yet God seemingly was inattentive, doing nothing. God was teaching him to rest in His appointments and to wait for His timing. Habakkuk's faith would be rewarded. He argues with God that His ways were incomprehensible and unjust. In the end Habakkuk had faith in Sovereign God that exceeded his circumstances and with confidence he said in Habakkuk 3:19, "The Sovereign Lord is my strength; He makes my feet like the feet of a deer. He enables me to tread on the heights."

I know I have lots of favorite songs: "Be *still* my soul: the Lord is on your side. Bear patiently the cross of grief or pain. Leave to thy God to order and provide. In every change He faithful will remain...Be still my soul: Thy God doth undertake to guide the future as He has the past. Thy hope, thy confidence let nothing shake; All now mysterious shall be bright at last..." (Katharina VonSchlegel)

"I wait for the Lord, my soul waits, and in His word I put my hope. My soul waits for the Lord more than watchmen wait for the morning ..." (Psalm 130:5-6)

When you are waiting, who you become while you are waiting is as important as what you are waiting for. God develops character in us over a lifetime. He's not in a hurry. He will satisfy the depths of our desire on His watch.

CHAPTER 17

Puzzle Pieces

The problem is that we always look for the missing piece of a puzzle instead of finding a place for the one in our hand.

—Alina Radoi

Our Father is the Master Planner and Designer. At times we ask Him for an immediate answer without realizing there are several puzzle pieces He still must fit into place. We may be ready to receive God's answer to our prayers, but we may have to wait until God fits other puzzle pieces together first.

We cannot set deadlines for the puzzle pieces to be placed in proper sequence—God does. I Peter 5:10b: "...after you have suffered a little while, He will himself restore you and make you strong, firm and steadfast." God's help will come at just the right time. If we wait faithfully and patiently, He will *complete* us and make us what we ought to be. God's delay is not God's denial. Many quit praying too soon when they don't see an immediate answer. You might as well align with God's ways; don't quit praying. God is completely dependable. He will place that missing puzzle piece in His time.

During a May retreat to Galiano Island in the Strait of Georgia off Vancouver, we were putting together a Thomas Kinkade 500-piece puzzle with friends Walter and Lori. We persisted diligently, working on it for many hours. But alas, we finished the puzzle with one piece missing. We looked everywhere for that one missing piece with the same diligence we invested in putting it together. It really disturbed me that the picture was not complete. I didn't want to give up and kept looking to no avail. Persistent is one thing I am! When could we realize the completion? I was actually fretting and worrying about it.

The next day in desperation I got on all fours under the table, feeling my way over every inch of the bright paisley rug. Voila! I found the missing piece upside down and totally camouflaged in the rug. I persisted and "felt" that the piece was somewhere awaiting the completion of a beautiful picture. A metaphor that God's whole picture plan was coming! Upon completion of the beautiful picture of the Thomas Kinkade fully lighted cottage, it invited me to enter in. Light with darkness encompassing the light invited us to enter that light.

One website I researched asked the question, "Are you missing a puzzle piece? Don't fret; we've got you covered!" Hmm, I knew God had us covered and would help us place that missing piece in His time so that the entire picture would be complete. Another website, seriouspuzzles.com, told of a step-by-step process to obtain that "dastardly, dishonorable missing piece!" If you've encountered the horror of the realization that your beloved puzzle is nearing completion, all except for a MISSING PIECE (their emphasis), there are actual steps to follow. The website then laid out the steps! Who knew? There is a science to lost puzzle pieces.

One site even told of fabricating a puzzle piece to complete a picture. But that makes the picture flawed or defective. That really doesn't work well. We cannot force God's hand in the sequences of life. It would not be for our best. I noted with interest some other sites like masterpieceinc.com and jigsawdoctor.com. Who is the masterpiece Designer? The jigsaw Doctor? The Designer Doctor to help complete the picture/plan! I cannot force or fabricate completion if a piece is missing, until He restores me as I Peter 5:6 and 7 in *The Message* indicates! "So be content with who you are, and don't put on airs. God's strong hand is on you; He'll promote you at the right time. Live carefree before God; He is most careful with you."

"The hardest pieces of a puzzle to assemble are the ones missing from the box." (Dixie Waters) Sometimes the process isn't logical. Socrates said, "The world's a puzzle; no need to make sense of it." I would add that the world's a puzzle if lived apart from God.

Just as puzzle pieces of our lives have to be assembled, so we all need *each other* to complete a beautiful picture. "We were given to one another by the Lord of the Body, because each one of us has a unique something to contribute—a piece of the divine puzzle no one else on earth can supply." (Charles Swindoll) Wonderful people in our lives helped us write our story and complete the picture.

Meredith Andrews, in her composition called *Pieces*, writes about a complex puzzle called life that wears you down—a constant fight. Feeling like you're alone and don't belong, don't measure up or won't be loved. Her lyrics speak about broken pieces, wearing scars, wounds, bruises. Because you belong to someone greater than all past mistakes and failures you don't have to hide in the dark, but rest in who He is because it is He who knows how to make the pieces fit. After all, He cares about every detail, every puzzle piece, even to numbering the hairs on our head. (Matthew 10:30)

Day by day, we learned to rest and wait for the pieces to fit together. Isaiah 14:24 from *The Message* instructed: "Exactly as I planned, it will happen." Worry was fruitless; it wasted our limited emotional resources. "Worry is a spasm of the emotion; the mind catches hold of something and will not let it go. It is useless to argue with the mind in this condition." (Winston Churchill, *Nash's Pall Mall Magazine*, 1925) It empties us of today's strength and our problems will still be there tomorrow. Worry is the antithesis of trust as we refuse what is given to us. It betrays a lack of trust in God's care and it is sin. God delights to lend His strength when we trust Him.

CHAPTER 18

Detoured

Sometimes it takes a sudden unexpected detour or wrong turn to get you to the right place.

—MANDY HALE

SOMETIMES THE DETOURED roads and routes are complicated and devastating, adding time to the journey. We begin an excursion without knowing where we're going. The unexpected route can end up confusing us at first, but it can be freeing and can become clear in time. I wanted to take the first exit I could find, but farther down the road I wouldn't want to trade this path I was on for the world. "If I've learned anything, it's that sometimes the most scenic roads in life are the detours you didn't even mean to take." (Angela N. Blount, *Once Upon A Roadtrip*)

Author and therapist Dan Allender writes of the mystery of God's disruptive intrusions providing what we need rather than what we want. His methods are unpredictable, paradoxical. He is the eternal artist who sculpts inscrutable situations. He invites us to trust and know Him in ways we could not apart from the mystery. He accomplishes His will without our seeing what lies ahead. But it is possible to flow with and participate in the marvel of the mystery. Though He is sometimes mysterious, His purposes are for us to form His image in us. God's plans are greater than our detours and wrong turns. Psalm 56:9 reminds us that God is on our side when our spirits are crushed and broken. He longs to help us.

Paul's dream to go to Rome to preach Jesus to Caesar spoke to my heart. We all know from Acts 27:37-44 what happened. Paul set sail for

Rome in chains but He knew he was being sent by the Spirit to bring the good news of Jesus Christ to the Romans. Then, a great storm hit as if to thwart God's purposes. He got shipwrecked on Malta as the ship hit a reef. Detoured! To the victims, Paul and 200 sailors who washed up on Malta, it seemed like a terrible experience. As if that was not enough, a viper came out of wood as they built a fire for warmth in the cold rain-storm and it bit Paul. Imprisonment, shipwreck, snake bite...where was God in all of this?

Paul did not die from the snake bite, but He had to speculate about the promises of provision and protection. Those awful experiences gave Paul the opportunity to minister grace and healing to the people on that island. Paul didn't know where this island was, but God did. God plans our Maltas! We are not comfortable with this idea that He sometimes orders and orchestrates our detours and pain. Sometimes we need a change of pace to jolt our perspective back into focus. A solitary island certainly would be a perspective changer. Only when God gets our attention can recovery begin. We can even be used of God in the middle of our Maltas.

There is an appointed time for everything (Ecclesiastes 3:1-3) and God doesn't waste those times. He sometimes causes them. Psalms 107:25 says that He commands and raises the stormy wind. I felt like I had landed on Malta during a storm. Malta seemed barren, lonely, desperate, and isolated, but its therapy was solitude, quietness, renewal, refreshment, healing and recovery which *take time*.

Christians are not comfortable with the idea that God allows or even causes storms in the lives of His people. Sometimes we are in storms of our own choosing and of our own making, and God lets us proceed so that we can learn that He forgives and rescues us even when we are in trouble by our own choice. Storms are of God whether we create them by our sinful nature and choices, whether the devil attacks us and creates a storm for us, or whether God designs a storm just to strengthen our roots in Him to teach us trust. "They come by His permission and with His approval," says David Jeremiah in *When Your World Falls Apart*. "These storms of our lives are not outside of His control. When we don't understand, we can still trust that God knows and has a purpose...The moment we accept the fact that our ordeal has been permitted, even intended by God, our perspective will change...Disruptive moments are simply Divine appointments...Progress without pain is usually not possible...Character and substance are shaped in the crucible of adversity. Pain makes us sensitive to God."

The detour is painful. The peril of the storm is often ominous and weighty as Psalm 107:26-27 in *The Message* articulates: "You shot high in the sky, then the bottom dropped out; your hearts were stuck in your throats. You were spun like a top, you reeled like a drunk; you didn't know which end was up." Your storm brings you to the bottom of your rope, your wits' end. When the storm is raging we don't know what to do. Prayer comes to mind! We become sensitized to God and His purposes. Storms, life-shaking situations, can be God's messengers to make Himself known in surprising and new ways. They may trigger a glimpse of God's glory. He has a way of wrapping His glory in painful problems and the mundane to give fresh revelation of Himself. Don't miss the message or God's glory. (Isaiah Chapter 6)

When things do not happen as we hoped, with confusing road blocks or detours on the journey, it likely means that God has Plan B for me. It could mean a completely different direction, a change of heart or attitude. But we don't need to struggle alone with Plan B. Trusting God with the situation will ultimately, in His time, bring that alternate plan to a good conclusion, releasing me to look more like Christ. Smith Wigglesworth said, "The power of God will take you out of your own plans and put you into the plan of God." Trusting God with the change of plans will enlarge our creative skills as we wait to see the end of the parade, the detour, or reason for the change.

Charles Spurgeon said, "I bear willing witness that I owed more to the fire and the hammer and the file, than to anything else in my Lord's workshop. I sometimes question whether I have ever learned anything except through the rod. When my schoolroom is darkened, I see most."

Then there was Brook Cherith! Years ago I had picked up the book *Elijah: A Man of Heroism and Humility* by Chuck Swindoll, but had never actually read it. One of my grandsons is named Elijah and I thought maybe I could journal something of the Biblical Elijah for him. Some day he could learn about the prophet and perhaps he could be another special Elijah prophet! So I picked up the book and was reminded that I didn't really wish Elijah's life experiences on my Elijah! This prophet had some extremely deep trials and plenty of "boot camp" isolation time and being set aside at Brook Cherith, east of the Jordan.

In I Kings 17 Elijah had prophesied of years of drought and of no rain to wicked ruthless King Ahab. Nothing seemed to awaken Ahab's evil soul to the things of God. Elijah then feared for his life and God literally told him to flee to Brook Cherith, to hide out in the middle of nowhere, to be fed by the ravens by day and night and to drink from Brook Cherith in total seclusion—until the drought about which he prophesied would dry it up. How many years, Lord, might that be? How humbling that a gifted prophet of God would have to endure this long isolation. We sometimes don't know what place God has prepared for our next teaching moment. Brook Cherith could not have been pleasant for Elijah by any stretch of the imagination. Yet the ravens provided the daily food and the brook provided the water. Provision in isolation!

God promises, "I will make a way in the wilderness and rivers in the desert…for I give water in the wilderness, rivers in the desert, to give drink to my chosen people." (Isaiah 43:19, 20, *ESV*) Penelope Stokes, in her book *Beside a Quiet Stream*, says, "To witness the miracle of rivers in the desert, you have to be *in* the desert."

Swindoll concludes in the book:

1) We must be as willing to be set aside as we are to be used. (check)
2) God's direction includes God's provision. (check)
3) We must learn to trust God one day at a time; we have to experience Cherith before God gives us the next step. (ok, in process on that one…kind of like a missing puzzle piece)
4) A dried-up brook is often a sign of God's pleasure, not disappointment, a sign of God's acceptance, not judgment. (I'll take it!)

God desired to prepare Elijah for greater mission and accomplishment. God strips us of our pride, fear, and resentment at our Cheriths. Swindoll writes how we can then learn forgiveness, breaking through habits and attitudes formed during our busy years of active service, unrealistic expectations, success-oriented motives or intentions that feed our carnality. How humbling. It crushes us into who He intends us to be—oil, fragrant flowers, fine wine.

Elijah's next place of direction and learning experience after Brook Cherith was a place called Zeraphath where he asked a poor widow to give him a drink of water, his most basic of needs. The brook had eventually dried up at Cherith and he had walked a long way to Zeraphath, arriving parched, way beyond thirsty. Asking a needy woman for a drink of water! How humbling is that? The rest of the story was that Elijah prayed for provision for her and God supplied. Remember the flour and oil provision? But then her son died and Elijah raised him from the dead with God's power. You must read the rest of the story in I Kings chapters 16 and 17 and realize the strength of Elijah and what happened to King Ahab and his cohorts. Amazing! What a life of an adventurer prophet! Yet, he was set aside at the brook for a long time.

Considering what Elijah went through, we had it pretty cushy during our set-aside pit time. God was providing above and beyond what we deserved. Nehemiah 9:19-20 speaks of God's great compassion on us because He did not abandon us to the desert. He gave us good manna and his good Spirit to instruct us. Though it is difficult living on manna in isolation, God knows what He is doing. If He has us sidelined and out of action for a while, we just need to stay humble, flexible and listen to His voice and leading for the next step. Waiting on the next puzzle piece of the plan!

There are four more lessons in Elijah's life from Swindoll's *Elijah* book:

1) God's leading is often surprising; don't analyze it. It may not make any sense.

2) The beginning days are often the hardest days; don't quit. Don't panic. The adversary of our souls loves to derail us, discourage us, tempt us to quit.
3) God's promises often hinge on obedience; don't ignore your part. Our obedience precedes God's provision.
4) God's provisions are often just enough; don't fail to thank Him. Practice grateful contentment!

Ann Voskamp's book, *One Thousand Gifts*, focuses on gratefulness and thankfulness in every day circumstances. "Thanksgiving always precedes the miracle." I needed to practice grateful contentment in everyday things. Then, as soon as the Lord sees His image in me, the furnace cools and I am ready for the next series of events He has planned.

I was learning to lean on Jesus, praise Him for all that was past and trust Him for all that was to come. I knew the Lord would fulfill His purposes for us (Psalm 138:8). The waiting part was still difficult but I kept reading Scripture verses that affirm it was part of the plan. I knew we would get up again…fly…soar …dance on that box lid, opened and laid out.

CHAPTER 19

Forgiveness Begins

Forgiveness is the fragrance that the violet sheds on the heel that has crushed it.

—LOUIS ZAMPERINI, ALSO ATTRIBUTED TO MARK TWAIN

ONE DAY WAY back in March 2005 I came across Joyce Meyer on TV. Something she said just nailed me to the wall. "If you harbor unforgiveness toward someone who has hurt you, your faith won't work. It just hits a wall." Oh, my! I wanted my faith to be effective, strong, assuring. I was deeply convicted and laid with my face in the carpet in front of the TV and asked God to help me forgive those who hurt me. I asked forgiveness for my attitudes and knew a process was beginning toward forgiving others who had (maybe even unintentionally or unknowingly) hurt me. This was difficult to believe, but not impossible. My heart was changed at that moment.

The lack of forgiveness exacts a toll and zaps much of our energy and resources. "Being unable or unwilling to forgive means that you remain emotionally under the control of the person who wronged you." (Paula Rinehart) Exodus 20:5 talks about the sins of the fathers that are visited upon the children to the third and fourth generations. Unforgiveness can ricochet through the generations of a family like a golf ball down a long hallway. We sometimes can see recurring patterns of negative things happening to us—how the enemy has access into our family line. Ironically, we desperately want to break free from the pain of it all, but everything sticks.

A harbored wrong can control a life. It becomes what we feed off of and we can feel "full" in our misery. Lack of forgiveness is like a fog of confusion. The issues are obscured and no one knows quite how to proceed. We want to discuss our injustices and rehearse how others may have wronged us. It is too easy to yield to negative and judgmental thinking. There's a climate of resistance to let a wrong go, driving me to speculate if I will be victimized again.

Holding a grudge against someone only strengthens a grip of bondage to them. Beth Moore calls it "entanglement or enmeshment, being subject to someone you won't forget." In other words we take the person we won't forgive and really don't care to be near, and we "drag them around with us everywhere we go." It really is the last thing we want to do but we are doing it!

Resentment, bitterness and grudges can eventually cause preoccupation in your mind which allows no release or relief. It is paralyzing for both you and the one you resent. Saint Augustine said, "Resentment is like taking poison and hoping the other person dies." Continuing to choose unforgiveness shows we are not grateful for God's forgiveness of our own shortcomings. It shows an indifference to the greatest thing God did for us and His purposes are interrupted in our lives. One could even lose the potential of an anointing. A self-righteous person does not forgive and that is a sin. There is no truth in us if we harbor bitterness or walk in darkness, which creates confusion in our minds and oppression in our hearts. (I John 1:6)

Ravi Zacharias' written words hit me: "An unwillingness to forgive locks us all up in bitterness, and throws away the key. It enslaves us to ingratitude, and chokes out gratefulness. It prevents us from experiencing the freedom that comes with free-flowing grace—both received and given—just as the ungrateful servant neither received nor extended grace in Jesus's parable. The ensuing desire to punish those who have hurt us belies our smug, moral superiority that designates punishment as more fitting than grace." I needed to maintain a grateful, forgiving heart, granting grace upon grace. Please help me, God!

"When we refuse to forgive we are setting ourselves up as a judge and demanding that others be perfect. That is something we cannot do.

When we judge we are usually predisposed to be unfair, negative and biased. God will judge and demand perfection of us when we judge others. We "play God" when we unfairly criticize or judge people. Luke 6:37 says, "Do not judge and you will not be judged. Do not condemn and you won't be condemned. Forgive and you will be forgiven." The degree to which we resist the enticement to judge will be the degree to which we ourselves are spared being judged. Judging is no badge of being more spiritual. (Isaiah 58:9-10; Colossians 4:6; I Peter 3:9) Satan is a thief who comes to steal, kill and destroy. (John 10:10) God is always fair and He knows the truth about us. The greater the sin committed that you must forgive, the greater measure of the Spirit that will come to you.

In the same way you judge others, you will be judged with the measure you use. The way you treat people is the way you will be treated. Don't criticize other's failures or faults. We seem to have keen vision to see shortcomings in others, yet are blind to our own. Judgment is rooted in hurt and bitterness.

If we accuse or point a finger, it could point back at us and God may even reveal bad things we have done. God can choose to discipline His children (I Corinthians 11:30; Psalm 103:10). God can likewise bless those who walk in humility and forgiveness. We inherit a blessing when we choose not to judge or insult. We cannot judge others' motives. We need to reserve judgment for God, because we value intimacy with the Father and fellowship with Him more than we desire judgment for anyone. Let mercy triumph over judgment (James 2:13). Because God has forgiven our great debt, we can forgive anyone who owes us anything or has hurt us in any way. We lay any injustice at the cross and let go of our claims for justice. Then Christ's grace and mercy can flow. Peace and joy will result. In repentance we are released into great freedom to fulfill God's plan for us. Then astonishment and promise await us at every turn. God will untangle all the pain as we remain in the grace place.

"See to it that no one falls short of the grace of God and that no bitter root grows up to cause trouble and defile many." (Hebrews 12:15) Eugene Peterson says it this way, "Work at getting along with each other and with

God. Otherwise you will never get so much as a glimpse of God. Make sure no one gets left out of God's generosity. Keep a sharp eye out for weeds of bitter discontent. A thistle or two gone to seed can ruin a whole garden in no time." I totally understand this parallel because I've been fighting thistles in my vegetable garden for a few seasons now. Romans 12:19: "Do not take revenge, my friends." Seems simplistic, doesn't it? Or not? People can misjudge our aims and tend to blame, say we are wrong, but they are not the judge. It is Christ.

I was amused with the truth of Matthew 7:1-5 from *The Message*, "Don't pick on people, jump on their failures, criticize their faults—unless, of course, you want the same treatment. That critical spirit has a way of boomeranging. It's easy to see a smudge on your neighbor's face and be oblivious to the ugly sneer on your own. Do you have the nerve to say, 'Let me wash your face for you,' when your own face is distorted by contempt? It's this whole traveling road-show mentality all over again, playing a holier-than-thou part instead of just living your part. Wipe that ugly sneer off your own face, and you might be fit to offer a washcloth to your neighbor."

Luke 6:37b-38 in the same Bible version says almost the exact same thing as the verses from Matthew 7. It ends with, "Be easy on people; you'll find life a lot easier. Give away your life; you'll find life given back, but not merely given back—given back with *bonus* and *blessing*. Giving, not getting, is the way. Generosity begets generosity."

The dictionary definition of forgiveness is 1) The act of excusing a mistake or offense and 2) A quality by which one ceases to feel resentment against another for a wrong he or she has committed. Forgiveness is not passivity but takes fortitude, backbone and divine power. Beth Moore likens it to the force that kept Christ nailed to the cross. Mahatma Gandhi affirmed that the process of forgiving is not for the faint of heart: "The weak can never forgive. Forgiveness is the attribute of the strong." Forgiveness is difficult, but it could be the one thing that will dissolve the hardness in my heart. It is a key to blessing. Repentance and forgiveness open up our hearts to allow the river of God's grace to flow freely in us.

A higher, Godward motivation to forgive is to avoid grieving the Holy Spirit. R. T. Kendall says when we grieve the Spirit we lose our presence of mind and it corrupts us and sets the whole course of our life on a downward path. We will not receive God's forgiveness without also forgiving others. If we refuse to do our part, we cut ourselves off from God's part. Matthew 6:15 reads: "If you do not forgive men their sins, your Father will not forgive your sins." How much better when I forgive and bless others as they want to be forgiven and blessed? "Do not grieve the Holy Spirit of God, with whom you were sealed for the day of redemption." (Ephesians 4:30)

In *The Message*, the same text and following reads: "Don't grieve God. Don't break His heart. His Holy Spirit, moving and breathing in you, is the most intimate part of your life, making you fit for himself. Don't take such a gift for granted. Make a clean break with all cutting, backbiting, profane talk. Be gentle and sensitive with one another. Forgive one another as quickly and thoroughly as God in Christ forgave you."

"The past is not changed by forgiving, but it does enlarge the future. We do not get over loss; we reconcile with it…The most creative power given to the human spirit is the power to heal the wounds of a past it cannot change. Then what happens to the people we forgive depends on them." (journal notes from Paul Boese)

Forgiving does not erase the bitter past. "A healed memory is not a deleted memory. Instead, forgiving that which we cannot forget creates a new way to remember. We change the memory of our past into a hope for our future." (Lewis Smedes)

It is a wise and chosen privilege to forgive. "A man's wisdom gives him patience and restraint; it is to his glory to overlook an offense." (Proverbs 19:11, *AMP*) "When we forgive, we see through other people's behavior to their need. We won't find justice in this world so give up the fruitless search for it and give mercy to those who wounded us. I must choose to forgive even if I don't feel like it. In remembering my own need for forgiveness can I choose to forgive others." (*Life is Tough, But God is Faithful* by Sheila Walsh)

"Not only refuse to keep a record of our wrongs, refuse to keep a record of our 'rights' and successes. Self-exaltation is wrong. I don't want anyone to be afraid of me or intimidated by me. And once God has forgiven me, He doesn't want me to be afraid of Him. God wants to put us at ease in His presence." (Charles Swindoll) "There is no fear in love. But perfect love drives out fear..." (1 John 4:18) The mark of true maturity is when somebody hurts you and you try to understand their situation instead of trying to hurt them back.

A. W. Tozer talked about letting go and being released from self-sufficiency, self-pity, self-absorption and self-hatred. "Letting go means freedom from the everlasting burden of always having to get our own way. Having to stay in control." In recognizing the subtle stranglehold of control, in relaxing my grip on the steering wheel, my heart is ready for the real life adventure of actively trusting God and letting offenses go.

We can forgive ourselves as we allow God to help us forgive others. I still knew God would turn our situation around for a blessing. "God gives beauty for ashes, strength for fear, gladness for mourning, peace for despair." Crystal Lewis' lyrics washed over me.

Then I picked up another helpful book on forgiveness and learned that there are stages of the journey involved in the forgiving process. The deeper the wound, the longer the process. I rediscovered that the people I need to forgive are human too. "Waiting for someone to repent before we forgive is to surrender our future to the person who wronged us. We set the prisoner free; and realize that he/she was me! We must surrender our right to blame or get even. We cannot avoid the pain altogether, but God does a process of healing the pain. Ultimately we desire the grace of God to them and wish them well. Only then, as we forgive, can we walk in stride with a forgiving God." (notes from Lewis Smede's *Art of Forgiving*)

God's redemptive work requires a great deal of time and space. It is a journey, and in the ongoing forgiving and healing process we can become more compassionate and real. It was a time of rebuilding identity and joy could thrive again. We were able to help others who were struggling to understand that they could also survive. It is helpful to talk with or read the story of someone who has walked this road before and one who has reconnected again with life. This is my desire to this day—helping others through pain, wounding and loss. God has been good to allow me to grant love, help and grace to those in need or who have experienced loss of any kind. And to forgive those who hurt me.

What if I forgive and bless in proportion to how you want me to forgive and bless you? "So, chosen by God for this new life of love, dress in the wardrobe God picked out for you: compassion, kindness, humility, quiet strength, discipline. Be even tempered, content with second place, quick to forgive an offense. Forgive as quickly and completely as the Master forgave you. And regardless of what else you put on, wear love. It's your basic, all-purpose garment."(Colossians 3:12-14, *MSG*) "God desires to reveal to us that His capacity to forgive is bigger than our capacity to sin." (A. W. Tozer) If we choose a life of love we will understand as Mother Teresa wisely understood, "If you judge people you have no time to love them." Ah, to possess and give that kind of love!

The love of God compels us and motivates us to love others. "Christ's love has moved me to such extremes. His love has the first and last word in everything we do…We don't evaluate people by what they have or how they look...God uses us to persuade men and women to drop their differences and enter into God's work of making things right between them." (II Corinthians 5:14, 16, 20, *MSG*)

In the last chapter of this book, entitled *Bene Dictus*, there are lists of helpful suggestions regarding consequences of an unforgiving spirit and tools for a life of forgiveness. We all can learn and grow in these models of forgiveness.

I've been absorbed by Louis Zamperini's life story after seeing the movie *Unbroken*. What a life of forgiveness. God has spoken to me through that movie regarding my own need to forgive. I cannot begin to fathom the depth of forgiveness prisoner-of-war Louis Zamperini ultimately granted "the Bird" and his other camp guards who continually beat him nearly to death, while being interred in Sugamo, a Japanese prison camp during WWII. It is incomprehensible how anyone could survive what he suffered and still desire a face-to-face meeting to grant forgiveness to the Bird and others who brutally beat him.

(Go to awesomestories.com/asset/view/FORGIVENESS-Unbroken-Louis-Zamperini-Story to read just one piece that the movie did not include as the end of the story.)

Franklin Graham documented parts of the story the movie missed. Louis Zamperini personally shares some of his own story. He has passed away but his story lives on. How could I even begin to consider that kind of love and forgiveness? Love is a key ingredient to forgive. "There is no love without forgiveness and there is no forgiveness without love." (Bryant H. McGill)

I needed the smallest amount of mustard-seed faith and renewed hope that everything would be alright as I forgave. Marilyn Meberg writes, "Hope is defined as a confident expectation. That means I haven't got what I'm hoping to get yet, but I'm expecting it any day now." Anything is possible with faith. He can even move mountains from here to there. Yes, God was giving me eyes to see His care in the details of everyday life, in my circumstances, and in total forgiveness.

CHAPTER 20

Moving On

Life is about savoring the current thing and then moving on to the next thing.

—Rick Porter

Rick generally had an uncanny character trait that allowed him to live in the moment, enjoy it, and when the time came to have to give that up or move on, it was not that difficult for him. It was easier for him to leave for the next place of ministry than for me. He could enjoy any place and then leave it. I would agonize over every move and relocation, wrestling with what I was leaving behind and agonizing over the uncertainly of the journey ahead! I would brood over "is this the perfect true will of God—this new place?"

Rick always knew for certain of God's direction before I would be drawn in or certain. Letting go of earthly things and close relationships and memories—not my cup of tea! It was necessary for me to desire to remain connected with friends from a former place. For Rick, his fresh vision ahead in a new place would remain his focus without looking back and it would begin immediately upon arrival in a new location. He lived more in the today and present. For me, not so easy! He had a prophetic way of knowing where he was to go and what he was to do. He would then put his nose to the grindstone, managing the new marathon experience from the get-go. Elizabeth Elliot said, "Wherever you are, be all there." Open wide to receive. No use in getting all knotted up about tomorrow, whether sorrow for what is gone, worry, or pounding regrets. Rather, live in the moment where God is.

So here is an amazing "writing on the wall" sequence of events in my story, albeit confusing initially. Nearly two years into our isolation with no job in sight, a stranger came to our door in Abbotsford, British Columbia. He asked us what happened to the **FOR SALE** sign in our front yard. I questioned, "What?" He replied that he had driven by our house the day before and had seen a for sale sign in our yard. I said, "Nnnoooo!" This, in a long, extended and drawn-out sing-songy voice swooping progressively upward! "There has never been a *for sale* sign in our yard!" He seemed puzzled, like he didn't believe me. Trying to process what I had just heard and being a bit tenuous and skeptical, yet euphoric, I told him to wait and I'd go get my husband. My reaction as I write this is about the same as I experienced at that moment. Total shock! What in the world? Had God allowed him to *see* a sign that was never there? Did God send him? I could not breathe! Total disbelief! I ran to get Rick. The man then told Rick that as they drove by our home the day before, he and his wife thought our house would be perfect for what they needed in the city and that there was a perfect parking area adjacent to our garage for his big RV. The FOR SALE sign had drawn them to our house. What? Their new business was right down the street from our home. He said our location was perfect!

Rick had a conversation with him, setting him straight and injecting that we just might consider selling our home even though it was not currently for sale since we had no place to go or to move. We figured maybe we should get a realtor immediately. Was God preparing us for this moment? The man wanted to walk through our house but we were uncertain about that. It all seemed rather strange. Too good to be true? Another detour?

As I was listening I wondered what we should do. Where would we go? We had no place to go. Yet I knew "the very steps we take come from God. Otherwise, how would we know where we were going?" (Proverbs 20:24, *MSG*) We immediately called our dear friend and realtor, Walter Funk, to inquire what we should do!

We think we should know where and when God is leading us. If we just get out the compass and map, read the directions, chart the course, we would figure it out. We want to know. We want God to speak clearly and plainly, telling us our destination up front so we can get on with business. Aren't we supposed to discern what to do and where He is leading because we have the mind of Christ? Shouldn't it be simple? It still didn't seem like it to me. Maybe this random man would make the next step of our journey clear. The two years of uncertainty and grasping for any straw of direction could become clear. Was another puzzle piece being located and positioned for our next step? We were expectant, trusting the "immortal, invisible, God only—wise."

The man brought his wife back and together they looked through our home and said they loved it and offered, in addition, to buy most of our furniture and furnishings to go with it! Oh, my goodness! How would we have moved it all back to the States anyway? Our belongings were old and mostly given to us in the first place. Nothing was of any great value to us and I was attached to almost nothing except some special art on my walls (gifts from wonderful artists in our church) and my Yamaha grand piano. We ventured that this was a miracle from the hand of God. Who would want my second hand mismatched furniture? Unreal! I must have had a puzzled crazy smirk on my face, eyebrows scrunched, my mind searching for direction.

However, after sitting down and conversing with the couple, the man made an offer that was just not even in the realm of satisfactory; yet his story tugged at our heartstrings! We were really confused. Had not God miraculously sent him our way? Why would a complete stranger want to buy our house? If we had trusted God up until now, we would continue to trust Him to reveal His purposes. But at that point I kind of wanted to punch a hole in the wall. My emotions were not unlike Paul's Malta tempest swells.

What happened to this miracle I had believed was of God? Our realtor said we needed to hold out for a much better offer and I was really tangled in confusion. Was even God pulling our string? Another one of those conundrums I may never understand? My stomach felt sick. We turned down the mystery buyer and immediately retained our friend as our realtor.

There had been no sign in our yard. But perhaps the man who "saw" a sign was sent as a sign. He did not convince us to sell, but he convinced us to list the house for sale. That is, to get a sign in the yard. Now everything seemed to proceed fast-paced. No *waiting* any longer! "Subito" (musical term) meaning *suddenly*! Our waiting was suddenly over!

The very next afternoon, at about 3 p.m., a **FOR SALE** sign was truly pounded into our front yard near the bing cherry trees by friend Walter! Within TWO hours, our Indo-Canadian neighbor across the street came over. He said he was very interested in buying our house for his extended family and to use our basement suite as a rental unit. WOW! He took a walk through the house along with our realtor friend and put in a full price offer on the spot. All this just two short hours after the *for sale* sign went up! He also said that some of my décor was lovely and would be appealing to his wife. He wanted to purchase that too. Could this really be happening? We had a full price offer and an offer to purchase the window treatments and some of the fragile stuff. This included a large pedestal dried hydrangea arrangement, in front of our entryway spiral staircase, that would not survive a move. (I did love that huge arrangement that was so inviting just inside our front door.)

His wife came across the street when she arrived home from work. This was the real test. She was doing her walk through. She drove a hard bargain on some décor. This south Asian woman told me at that time that the three single candolier lights in my front windows that I kept lit 24/7 had blessed her every night when she arrived home after dark. It somehow was meaningful to her. I had prayed over the years that we would be a light emanating to our neighborhood which was culturally diverse. The candles in the bay window represented my heart's desire and prayer.

Our neighbors were from Guatemala, Holland, Fiji, India and England, to name a few. Those perpetual lights symbolized my prayer to be a light to all who would see it. That Jesus would be high and lifted up for all to see. The Light of the World! Her word of appreciation of my window lights confirmed my heart's desire and prayer—and to someone likely of a Sikh background.

Right down the main street of town and a block or two from Sevenoaks were two imposing Sikh temples. Everyone had to drive between the two temples with spires rising to the sky to get to most places in town. Abbotsford had the third highest proportion of visible minorities in Canada after Toronto and Vancouver. About 20% in our town were South Asian; most were of the Sikh religion. These people migrated to the area in 1905 to work the land and orchards around the city. There were numbers of temples around town. But the lighted cross over our church shown brighter. May the name of Jesus be lifted high! May the candoliers, to this day shining from my front window in Iowa, shine the light of Jesus to all who see them.

We occasionally had Sikhs visit our church and they were known to present gifts of produce, vegetables and candles on the platform during the service or after church. We have some amazing stories that still blow me away today of our times of ministering to Sikhs. We had a Pakistani woman on our outreach staff and our last youth pastor was a friend and neighbor, also of East Indian descent. Those wonderful neighbor friends would be the last to help us pack our house and clean and wave goodbye to us as we left Abbotsford for the last time. They also received some of our frozen bing cherries! Thank you Emil and Wendy and family!

Within about a *day* of selling our home and wondering where in the world we should now go, Rick was offered a job as Development Director (later to become Executive Director) of the Okoboji Bible Conference in Arnolds Park, Iowa. It is located in the northwest part of the state in the beautiful Okoboji Lakes resort area. We had been a part of this conference for many previous years—Rick as director and I had been the conference pianist for 37 or more years. I started playing there as a teen. It was a place we had both attended every summer of our lives from infancy (in utero, if you want the real truth)! No matter where we lived or served in the United States or Canada, we would attend the conference and participate every summer. Okoboji was home regardless of our zip code.

This special place began in 1935. My grandkids are the fifth generation on my dad's side to attend this annual summer gathering of Christians of all descriptions. Dad's parents attended. In fact, my Grandfather actually pastored an early Christian and Missionary Alliance Church in Spirit Lake, the town in which we now live, from September 1949 until early 1951. I only learned this a few years ago. We really were returning to our roots! Rick's dad and my dad were both board members of the conference association in earlier days. Rick and I had met at the conference as kids! Our first date as teens was at this conference! He was from Omaha and I was from the small town of Mountain Lake, in Southwest Minnesota.

The job in Iowa seemed right and tailored for us. Everything suddenly seemed to be falling into place according to God's perfect plan. Besides, I would be near my parents, all my siblings, and one daughter and family all living in Minnesota. This was perfect timing and a good job. We had a long history with this ministry. The next puzzle piece! Let the generations hear and rejoice!

I had missed family connection all our years in ministry across the United States and Canada. I had felt sad that my parents could not see our kids, their grandkids, grow up. Yet, we ourselves, living in Canada, were distanced from our own children and their families in Boise, Idaho, Junction City, Oregon, and Crown College in Southwest suburban Minneapolis, Minnesota. Living in Iowa would be even farther away from our west coast kids. God was redirecting our steps and we would trust.

Knowing we had a new place and season of ministry, we immediately went into packing mode. Several friends came to help. Our praying intercessor friend came to completely pack up a bedroom and bathroom upstairs. Thanks, Pam! Others came to clean behind us. A garage sale helped sell some furniture and household items. Our Family Life pastor, Rita, came to help pack all my special dishes and china, marking them FRAGILE!

The very sad part for me was getting rid of boxes of piano and choral music I had collected over many years of serving in the church. Teaching piano since I was a teen meant lots of accumulated music. I just celebrated my 50th year of teaching. I won't forget the back of a pick-up truck loaded high with boxes of music to be hauled to the junk heap. Moving and getting rid of things I considered precious and valuable was difficult for me in each move we made. My heart hurt! Oh Lord, help me release and let go! Tears flowed! That was always the hardest part of our many moves for me.

My last views of majestic Mt. Baker lingered. This snowy peak, just across the border from us, greeted me each sunny morning through the sliding glass door to the deck off our bedroom.

I would miss my home and the beauty of the area, the ocean and mountains, the mild winters, our good friends and many who loved and believed in us and interceded in prayer for us. I would so miss worshipping at our former church (fantastic musicians ministered to me every week—and I still miss it to this day). I'd miss beautiful Vancouver Island, the lighted Parliament building at night, breath-taking Butchart Gardens which tourists flocked to view and ferry trips to Lonsdale Quay for shopping. We had taken for granted the magnificent musical productions at the Queen Elizabeth Theater and others. Just south, in the Skagit Valley near LaConner, Washington we enjoyed trips to see the miles of tulips and daffodils dressed in brilliant color with the backdrop of the mountains. British Columbia offered seafood bistros along the ocean piers in which to dine while watching the fishing boats come and go. We would buy any variety of seafood as fresh as fresh can get along the docks. The graces abound. The Empress Hotel in Victoria on Vancouver Island, slow ships and fast ferries coming and going, our numerous trips to quaint Whistler up in the mountainous ski areas. We experienced this, thanks to friends who gave us use of their condo. Yachting on the ocean! And the Cultus Lake retreat house! Sometimes it never got any better than that! I would miss it all! Even our States' families on rare visits would benefit from gracious people gifting us with opportunities that we could not have had the resources to provide. Beautiful memories! Beautiful places! Beautiful friends!

Just as I finished packing the last music I could not part with, a lady dropped over to our house. The Haddads had occasionally attended our church. She presented me with a deep cranberry red handmade prayer shawl and a navy blue one for Rick. She said she had already prayed over them while she made them and encouraged us to use those prayer shawls in our new place as we would beseech God for needs and praise Him for all He had done and was yet to do. Like God covering us with His feathers, I would wear my prayer shawl and feel His protection and continued provision and He would hear my petitions. I still have my shawl on our black leather chair to this day. I am on occasion praying for the needs of others close and far away with the shawl draped around me. How would she know deep red is my favorite color? Thank you, Rose-Marie.

Another thing that absolutely blew me away was the last minute gift of a beautiful work of carved art that a young man in his twenties in the church crafted with his own hands and brought over just before we moved. He gifted us with a large white smoothly polished marble sword carved out of one piece of marble and mounted on a beautifully finished board over three feet long with a verse from the Psalms hand-carved below the sword. I've never seen such carving talent from such a young man. It was beautiful and he had put so much time and work into it. I tear up as I remember and see his gift around our house as a reminder of God our Defender. We would continue to be warriors for Christ wherever we went. Thank you, Mirko! An amazing gift! What an insightful, gifted, Spirit-led young man!

A visual that popped into my head as I picture Mirko's white marbled sword wall art is a verse from Revelation 19:11-16 about the Warrior Christ, "I saw heaven standing open and there before me was a white horse, whose rider is called Faithful and True (the rider is Christ returning as Warrior-Messiah-King). With justice he judges and makes war. His eyes are like blazing fire and on his head are many crowns. He has a name written on him that no one knows but he himself. He is dressed in a robe dipped in blood and his name is the Word of God. The armies of heaven (angelic beings and perhaps believers) were following him, riding on white horses and dressed in fine linen, white and clean. Out of his mouth comes a sharp sword with which to strike down the nations. He will rule them with an iron scepter. He treads the winepress of the fury of the wrath of God Almighty. On his robe and on his thigh he has this name written: KING OF KINGS AND LORD OF LORDS." (parentheses mine) Can you imagine or envision that? Now that sword has impact—as does the Rider of that horse!

Packing now completed, our son-in-law Aaron from Boise had come to help us load and drive one of our two rental trucks over the border and to our new location in Iowa. We would stop in the Boise area on the way to pick up daughter Vonda and grandson Timothy for the trip. What fun. What a blessing! I took final photos of our former house and beautiful neighborhood and we waved goodbye to the last faithful enduring friends who were there to see us drive away. I still can see our dear friends waving us on—the journey proceeding—up the street and toward the border. God continued to lead and guide us into new places. I finished recording a Christmas CD in late 2014 that my daughter helped me appropriately title, *STILL PROCEEDING*!

One thing I've learned about life: it goes on! We are still ever proceeding! God guiding the way! Paul Anka once said, "I've always believed that if you don't stay moving, they will throw dirt on you!" It now seemed easy and hard. Happy to have a place to go was good, but the sad and difficult part was what we were leaving behind.

As we drove toward the border in our loaded truck, we heard Brian Doerksen singing on the radio, *Lead Us Lord*! The crossroads! I shook my head as my eyes widened and mouth dropped open. We could hardly believe what we were hearing! I'm breaking into tears even as I re-live this moment, recalling God's faithfulness. The Father was singing the same affirmation over us again in an intimate moment.

Crossroads, now with new direction and leading. It's time to dream again! Time to risk again! What a blessing and confirmation at the right moment. Thank you God and Brian!

Back over the border crossing and the scrutiny of border guards for the last time! Praise God! It seemed too easy this time! Moving into Canada had been an absolute nightmare at the border crossing for us. It just was unbelievable and I won't rehearse the bizarre craziness. It is a book of stories in itself! How could it have gotten any better than this now on the return?

Moving on means you accept what happened and continue living. You go on. "I can choose to let what happened define me, confine me, refine me, outshine me, or I can choose to move on and leave it behind me." (unknown)

This is a story! This is God's faithfulness! I want generations to come to know His faithfulness. Hear and rejoice!

CHAPTER 21

Going Home

Now get yourselves ready. I'm sending my Angel ahead of you to guard you in your travels, to lead you to the place that I've prepared. Pay close attention to Him. Obey Him.

—Exodus 23:20, MSG

Exodus 23:20 was written on a recipe card, positioned on my refrigerator for years. Take time to read the entire context of this verse. Included are the benefits of obeying His direction and paying close attention—even to the blessing of food and water. He would ***rid our sicknesses*** and make sure we lived full and complete lives. He promised He would fight for us and lead us to a new land. We were getting ourselves ready for the new place He had already prepared.

The trip from British Columbia to Iowa was long. We hoped that our trucks would not overheat in the mountains. Diesel fuel prices were at an all-time high due to Hurricane Katrina. It took over $200 for each fill-up and this for two trucks! With each mile, our wallets became lighter, but so did our hearts! We had a place to go, a job to do and dreams to dream again. My concern also was how my grand piano would take the bumps. It did just fine. Just a little scratch on the lid. Character.

We moved temporarily into furnished housing on the conference campus in Arnolds Park, Iowa until we could purchase a home in nearby Spirit Lake. Labor Day, September 4, 2005 was our unloading day with the help of new friends and conference people who showed up to help, along with our daughters and husbands. Our niece Tara and family, missionaries in Haiti, happened to be there for support and help. It felt good! We stored all our belongings in the old conference tabernacle on the campus. It took only one hour to unload and stack boxes and furniture on wood pallets where they would be stored until we could purchase a house.

A few days later, after wonderful family time (minus our son and family in Oregon), our kids flew back home to Boise, Idaho and our other daughter and family drove back home to Minneapolis, Minnesota.

I had met a new friend, Kathy Skalbeck, who told me she had been praying for *two* years that we would move to Spirit Lake, Iowa. I thought back. Ah! She began praying about the time we were released from our church in Canada. She had met us at Okoboji Conference a few years previously, but I honestly could barely remember meeting her. Rick had met her husband, Jeff, at the Sioux Falls airport some years before. Why would God direct her to begin praying two years previous to this that we would specifically move to Spirit Lake, Iowa? She had no idea of our situation. Another sparkling jewel! Confirmation!

As we got settled in our new job, we found a home in Spirit Lake. We looked at homes in towns very near the conference grounds, but ended up in Spirit Lake. Kathy's prayer had been specifically answered. People, a few whom I had never met, offered to paint several unacceptably gaudy-colored rooms in our home. Goodbye old friends. Hello new!

We teamed with some friends in our prayer/care group. Jeff and Kathy Skalbeck, Dave and Judy Graanstra (Judy is Rick's office administrator), and Dr. James and Kari Webb. They were *serious* bicyclers. Rick accepted a wonderful gift from the Webbs, an amazing bike, so Rick could join in cycling. He began to love it. His first big success was riding Tour de Kota with the group, a bicycle ride around the state of South Dakota.

In September I received a note from someone sharing the words of Marsha Burns who blogs on the site *Small Straws in a Soft Wind*. "Expect to resume progress in every area of life...Hope is once again restored... Do not be afraid to forge ahead with new vigor and strength of purpose."

I was ready for the new, the hope, the forging ahead, the risking and dreaming again.

After a few months in Iowa, I happened to be looking back at old emails for some reason. An email from a parishioner in our Canada church popped up, out of the blue. I barely had known her. I had met once in her home for a women's Bible study. I remembered we had prayed for her because she had been diagnosed with a malignant brain tumor. At the time I had no idea how prophetic her Scripture word would be—past and future.

Her email simply quoted Isaiah 58:8-12. Please read it slowly and thoughtfully. "Then your light will break forth like the dawn, and *your healing will quickly appear*; then your righteousness will go before you, and the glory of the Lord will be your rear guard. Then you will call, and the Lord will answer; you will cry for help, and He will say: Here am I. If you do away with the yoke of oppression, with the pointing finger and malicious talk, and if you spend yourselves in behalf of the hungry and satisfy the needs of the oppressed, then your light will rise in the darkness, and your night will become like the noonday. The Lord will guide you always; He will satisfy your needs in a sun-scorched land and will strengthen your frame. You will be like a well-watered garden, like a spring whose waters never fail. Your people will rebuild the ancient ruins and will raise up the age-old foundations; you will be called Repairer of Broken Walls, Restorer of Streets with Dwellings." Verses 8 and 9 in *The Message* say, "Your lives will turn around at once. Your righteousness will pave your way. The God of glory will secure your passage. Then when you pray, God will answer. You'll call out for help and I'll say, Here I am."

This had deep meaning and significance for me as I received it, but I had no idea how prophetic it would yet become. Our ministry, directly or indirectly, would include feeding the hungry (Community Table), housing the homeless on the campus, counseling the hurting, mentoring pastors, offering the *Perspectives* course, partnering with KJIA Christian radio, guiding teens with Timber Bay, supporting a community GriefShare program, the Prayer Center ministry, the summer Okoboji Bible Conference,

Rick's counseling services and preaching across all denominations, an international student work exchange...and on and on. No shortage of things to do or people to love. Here we are, Lord. Help us be the repairer of broken walls and people.

I would almost immediately begin a new part-time ministry of my own as relief house parent to pregnant unwed young women (mostly young teens) through Cherish House. What a ministry and beautiful home for these girls, and only a few short blocks from our home. I loved working with the girls, some who chose to parent and some who chose to place their babies for adoption, after intensive counseling, instruction and love. At one time our own home became a "shepherding home" for one of the girls who placed her baby for adoption and then came to live with us for six months. I continued the Cherish House ministry about seven years until my dad became very ill and needed care.

Beth's email took me to Isaiah 58:11 in *The Message* which reads, "I will always show you where to go. I'll give you a full life in the emptiest of places—firm muscles, strong bones. You'll be like a well-watered garden, a gurgling spring that never runs dry. You'll use the old rubble of past lives to build anew, rebuild the foundations from out of your past. You'll be known as those who can *fix anything, restore old ruins, rebuild and renovate, make the community livable again.*" (emphasis mine) That's all the email from Beth included—that Scripture. Wow! This is exactly what we would be doing! A new passion and call. Thanks Beth for that email.

I thought Isaiah 58 was a significant word from God, but it became obviously more prophetic after several months had passed.

CHAPTER 22

Something Dark

Darkness is often the setting for humanity's closest encounters with the Divine.

—*Unknown*

Be our light in the darkness, O Lord.

—*Book of Common Prayer*

"God sees in the darkness of troubled times as clearly as He does in the daylight." (Psalm 139:11-12) "We can rely on Him—He knows what will happen before we do; nothing in all creation is hidden from His sight." (Hebrews 4:13, paraphrased)

We want to avoid the perils of darkness at all costs, the danger of the night, the dark night of the soul. We want protection from the powers of darkness. "Darkness is a synonym for sin, ignorance, spiritual blindness and death." (Barbara Brown Taylor) We want the Lord to shine into our lives the brightness of His Holy Spirit. Where there is light there can be no darkness.

"Just as a jeweler lays a piece of black velvet across the counter upon which to display his precious gems, so the Lord is using the darkness of our circumstances and the world's situations as the backdrop to display His glory in us and His Church." (Dick Block)

Rick had spent years coughing. It was annoying! Perpetual! It was a hacking loud, dry cough. It began several years previous. By now I was just used to hearing it and attempting to ignore it. At night it was awful and would wake me up. It almost became a part of who he was, it seemed. I didn't understand the perpetual issue and it troubled me. I sensed something was not right for years.

Rick was invited to speak at retreats, churches, banquets, camps and events in the Midwest states and Florida. He took them all and represented Okoboji Conference well. One such event was coming up. I was concerned because Rick was looking more pale, tired and his cough seemed to be getting worse. I wasn't sure how he could endure days of speaking in several sessions each day. He was becoming increasingly more doubtful himself as his strength diminished.

One day Rick wrote a routine email update to the conference board of directors. In it he asked, "Please pray that the Great Physician would make a house call to our address." Rick sought an appointment with our physician friend but was told that it would be a week. Rick emailed his physician and asked if he could be seen sooner.

Before Rick would even arrive home from work that evening, our friend Dr. James Webb was waiting in our living room with his physician's satchel! With his stethoscope in his right hand and his left hand on Rick's lower back, Dr. Webb listened to Rick's lung and diagnosed, "You have right lung pneumonia." He continued curiously which I noted. He said something that Rick didn't even remember. He spoke of "some additional dark thing" in Rick's lower back where his left hand was touching. Some awareness from God to Dr. Webb? What did he mean? He prescribed antibiotics for pneumonia and followed up with an appointment at the office.

Dr. Webb wouldn't let up. He ordered x-rays for Rick's lungs and had a pulmonologist review them. The pneumonia seemed to be clearing up. Yet Dr. Webb was unrelenting, somehow knowing something was not right. He ordered a CT scan of Rick's lungs. The young technician decided to continue scanning lower than the lungs when she saw something questionable at the bottom of the scan. Her demeanor changed and she continued more and more positions and scans. Rick later told me that he noticed her change of tone even as he was informed that they would take additional scans. Later that day, Friday, April 21, 2006, Rick phoned Dr. Webb to inquire as to the outcome of the scans. Dr. Webb invited us to his home that evening to talk. Rick accepted but I could not go because

I had a previous church women's event scheduled that evening. A little while into the conversation, Rick asked the good doctor if the results of the CT scan had come back yet. Dr. Webb offered to take Rick into the living room and asked if he wanted me there to hear the results. Rick being Rick just said, "Give it to me." He said it was fine for Kari Webb to sit in as well.

Our doctor friend proceeded to tell Rick that he had advanced kidney cancer and that the renal cell carcinoma could possibly already have metastasized because it was so advanced and large. Dr. Webb could only conjecture that it could be terminal. What grim words! Rick's scans had been sent to Mayo Clinic in Rochester, Minnesota and Sioux Falls, South Dakota to be read by technicians and also to an area urology specialist. The question was, had it metastasized beyond the kidney? Was this why Rick was coughing so much for years? It seemed like a strange symptom for advanced kidney cancer. Could it yet have something to do with the lungs? Kidney cancer metastasized into the lungs?

When I got home from my evening event, Rick shared with me his sad news. We sat on our bed as Rick divulged the devastating, stark reality that we might be preparing for a tough battle that was not necessarily survivable. We both embraced and cried and prayed together. Yet our peace was inexplicable beyond our understanding. Both of us! It could have been some initial shock. Yet, somehow, God was incredibly carrying us. To this day, I cannot explain the peace we felt. Those were the hard facts and we would again trust God, the only thing we could do. Unlike a fog of confusion, that "dark thing" did not envelop us because God seemed close and active in the dark! More so at that point than ever.

We decided not to tell our kids yet until we had more details. We knew they would be completely unsettled, pained and devastated. We slept on the tough news.

The next morning, Dr. Webb called Rick to tell him that the urologist did not think the cancer had metastasized. Yet, not until after surgery and follow-up scans could we be certain.

Our caring group and bicycling friends gathered one day in our front yard in their spandex, helmets and with their bikes. Sitting on our front lawn on a beautiful afternoon, Dr. James explained Rick's diagnosis to our group and the uncertain prognosis. We all had a good cry. I have a photo of us sitting on the grass, hearing the diagnosis. We will always remember that moment.

Rick was told that he very likely had that huge kidney tumor for three or four years already. That goes back to the time we still pastored in our Canada church. No wonder he was so drained and coughed for so many years and his body was so tired and worn out. From way back! He had been to points of exhaustion and burn out in the last years in Canada. He would continually work *through* it. That's what Rick does. Tenacity! Dogged persistence and perseverance!

In addition Rick had perpetual pain in both his ankles. Over the years standing to preach was so excruciatingly painful that he could hardly think or put a sentence together without God's help and anointing. At one point he had gone through surgery to fuse one ankle with many pins to hold it together which left him with no range of motion. For a while he had to preach from a wheelchair and then a stool. He always walked with a limp. Yet, Rick always added, as Mephibosheth, that he sat at the King's table every day of his life. Read this great story in 2 Samuel Chapter 9. Verses 9 and 11 tell that even though Mephibosheth was crippled in both feet, he would dine at King David's table all the days of his life. David took him in as one of his own sons. Rick felt like Mephibosheth must have felt. When crippled feet are hidden under the table, one need not so much think about the disability as sweet food and drink!

This helps to understand Rick's physical condition at the end of our years in Canada. We did not know he already had cancer draining life away from him. No wonder everything seemed so formidable and daunting. His only obvious symptom was the perpetual cough and weakness.

More appointments were made; we sought the help of specialists in Spencer, Iowa. The day before Rick was to go speak for a number of days at a Christian and Missionary Alliance MidAmerica District pastors conference in Nebraska City, Nebraska, an appointment was made to learn more from a urologist and surgeon at a clinic in Spencer. We were actually all packed and the car loaded with our suitcases to leave from that very appointment to drive to Nebraska City for the speaking engagement. Could we emotionally do this? Would Rick have the strength to go through with several speaking sessions knowing what he was facing? Would more devastating news in that appointment result in immobilizing and undermining what Rick planned to speak to the district ministry attendees?

Arriving at the Spencer appointment, we both went into the urologist's office together that morning of April 24, 2006 not having any idea what to expect. The surgeon quite immediately informed us that it appeared from all reports that the cancer was confined to and in the kidney. He suggested surgery should occur on the first operating room table in the first hospital available. We could have it performed in Sioux Falls, Rochester Mayo Clinic, Minneapolis, or right there in the Spencer Hospital. Rick asked the surgeon, Dr. Christ (YES, that indeed was his name), when and where *he* thought it should happen. He replied, "The very *first* operating table you can get... We do kidneys on Thursdays." Rick said, "Let's go for it!"

Surgery would be in just three days, the very morning after we would return from the Nebraska retreat, April 27, 2006. We didn't know for sure what would be found as Rick was opened up. We had simple trust and faith. There still was small uncertainty if there had been any metastasis. Yet we knew God brought us to this point for a reason and He would not abandon us now. That simple!

As we exited the exam room that morning, we noticed multiple original paintings hanging on the walls in the waiting room. They were all originals by Dr. Christ's wife and they were signed "J. Christ." Her first name was Jane but she was Jesus to us! Somehow we knew God was in this all. It was providential and timely to even stop to look closely at the paintings on our way out the door! It made us rejoice with renewed hope!

We drove directly from that appointment to the pastors' retreat in Nebraska with heavy hearts but expectant for what God was going to do. For some reason, I had no fear. Neither did Rick. We were surprised later by our peace and calm. Few people knew Rick had been diagnosed with renal carcinoma. Our wounding in Canada seemed much harder than the cancer diagnosis. Hands down. Maybe we had learned how to trust and lean hard into God. I know that not everyone will understand this. But, it was true for us. Had we learned through hard times and in all things to trust in God...and found Him faithful? Yes and yes! I could then understand what my friend told me years before—that their removal from their church, also in Abbotsford, was much harder than learning she had possible terminal cancer. Ah! Unless you have walked in those shoes, you just don't know. There are many categories of pain and trials and each response to it can be different as well.

Rick spoke those days at the district conference on a series of messages, "Heads Up," he had written in response to our dark times and ways the enemy of our souls comes in to seek to destroy, divide and scatter God's people in His church in covert and overt ways. It was intense stuff, but his ministry was well received.

I was again wearing a more specialized Holter monitor for my racing heart while we were there for those retreat days. God ministered to Rick and me during that time and He gave us strength.

Before we finished the sessions at the retreat in Nebraska, the district superintendent invited both of us to be anointed and prayed for by the entire pastors and spouses group. Everyone had been informed during Rick's last session of his cancer and surgery to follow the very next morning. The leaders surrounded us, prayed for healing on us in the name of Jesus and anointed us with oil, as instructed in James 5:13-16.

I know beyond any shadow of doubt in that moment of anointing and prayers at the retreat on Wednesday, April 26, 2006, that I was instantly healed of my tachycardia while wearing the Holter monitor! It was the simplest of faith. Nothing dramatic. Just simple prayers of righteous men and women, a tiny bit of oil, and my small mustard-seed faith. I have not had any episodes since that time. After 26 years of that affliction! Praise our Healing Jesus! When I am reminded of my healing I take time to thank and praise God for His goodness to me. Some mornings as I awake I praise and worship God as I recall His amazing grace as my Rapha Healer! Let the generations hear and rejoice!

CHAPTER 23

Besor Gulch

Besor Gulch teaches us the important principle of grace, one that forces us to rethink and revolutionize our ministries as members of the body of Christ.

—*From Tragedy to Triumph, a study of I Samuel 30, Bible.org*

We arrived back home to Iowa from Nebraska later than we hoped on that April 26, Wednesday evening, later than Rick was supposed to begin to ingest his pre-surgery "cleaning out" drink. I was concerned how that night might "go!" Within a few hours he would be in the operating room in Spencer to have one kidney removed and anything else that looked suspicious. Our youngest daughter Nikki, from Waconia, Minnesota arrived to walk through this time with us. Our kids in Idaho and Oregon were praying from there as were many others.

Dr. Webb asked if he could himself drive Rick to Spencer Hospital for pre-op and surgery on that Thursday in 2006. Rick wondered if I'd be OK with that request. I was fine with that because he had to go so early in the morning for prep, and my car would be full with my daughter and my parents who would arrive from Minnesota to go to the hospital with me.

Arriving a bit later at the hospital, I saw Rick just before he went into surgery and committed him to God's care. Just simply. Faith that God still had Rick, my husband, in His big hands and knew as Sovereign God what was for our best. As he was going in to surgery I asked Dr. Webb if it seemed appropriate to take some photos, as I thrust my camera into his hands. Yeah, that's like me! Photos of everything! Even a huge, ugly, oversized, cancerous kidney! Dr. Webb had requested and was granted the privilege of scrubbing in and observing the surgery, as a friend and Rick's physician. Friends and a couple of pastors arrived before and during the surgery to wait with us in the waiting room, along with a couple of Okoboji Conference board members. Some of our care group arrived.

Urologists Christ and Mendenhall performed the surgery—a radical nephrectomy (total removal of a kidney). The pathologist was Roxy McLaren, who was a regular attendee and faithful supporter of the Okoboji Bible Conference. Dr. Webb was there to support and observe. Rick was surrounded with good care and God had everything in control. Dr. Webb later reported that the operating room was bathed in love.

The wait seemed long! Miracles sometimes take *time*! We grew restless in the *waiting* room. Waiting again! People came and went to show their support and pray. I was in total indescribable peace as I sat with family and friends. You know, from Philippians, "the peace of God which surpasses all understanding."

After the surgery Dr. Webb eventually came out to call my daughter and me into an adjacent room. He privately informed us that the surgery had gone well and the cancer was entirely contained in the kidney. The renal vein leading from the kidney had no evidence of metastasis. Praise God! Let the generations hear and rejoice!

Dr. Webb had taken photos of the mass they had removed. He showed them to Nikki and me. It looked gigantic. The photos shocked me. The entire kidney was dark and ugly. Layer upon layer like rings on an aged tree trunk. It was almost as if the *reproach* of what we had been through in the past and what the cancer represented was cut away—gone! Wow, God! Teach us what you desire in and through this! This massive cancerous kidney was removed maybe moments before metastasis! Let all the generations hear of God's faithfulness!

Those still in the waiting room were anxious because Dr. Webb, Nikki and I were in the consultation room too long they thought. Was there bad news? No, actually good news! Besor! That word means "good news," a grace place in the Bible. My favorite sermon Rick preaches on occasion now is entitled *Besor* from I Samuel chapter 30—for those who are too tired to go on. For those there is good news. I never tire of hearing the good news every time he preaches it. I sometimes have to request it again because I need to hear it again.

Besor is an amazing story of David and his 600 men at Ziklag, finding it burned, plundered and destroyed by the enemy Amalekites, their wives and children captured and taken away, and everything gone. When David and his men came to the Besor Ravine in pursuit of the enemy raiders, 200 of the 600 men were too tired to continue. They had plenty of motivation—their families needed to be rescued—but after marching to Ziklag they now were too exhausted to go after the enemy. Two hundred men collapsed there in the heat by Brook Besor. David and the other 400 men pressed on, leaving much of their gear behind with the 200 so they could expend less energy and move faster.

The bottom line of this Biblical story is that God gives grace and cares for those who are too tired to go on. And in the process, God brings exactly the right people into your path at the very time you need them to fulfill your needs and purposes. Read about the Egyptian! A man left for dead gave new life and clarity to David's pursuit. (I Samuel 30:11-15) I *love* this story. Besor! Good news! Dr. Webb was right in our path at just the right time to save Rick's life. From the beginning to the end! We were at Besor Ravine, Good News gulch, a low place that God turned into a highpoint!

Everything and everyone the Amalekites had taken from Ziklag was recovered and rescued in addition to the spoils of the enemy raids. Nothing was missing. David brought it all back. But then there was a problem about dividing the spoils of victory. The 200 who were too exhausted to continue on with the 400 fighting men wanted their part of the spoils too. The 400 who finished the battle victory didn't think the exhausted men should get a share of the loot. After all, *they* were the ones to take the credit for the victory and demanded they should be rewarded appropriately for winning the battle. They tried to usurp David's leadership. Yet David taught them a huge grace lesson in granting everyone the spoils, evenly distributed among the 600, because the battle was a team effort and the victory was granted to them by God himself. Grace means that we do not have to work for God's blessings, salvation or forgiveness. All we have to do is receive what we have not earned and for which we dare not take credit. David taught the principle of amazing grace. Besor!

Back in the waiting room, I wanted to shout, "Besor," but everyone was in total suspense and that might have scared them! Upon learning the good news, everyone in the waiting room joined hands in a circle and thanked God for His faithfulness and the outcome. The digital photos taken during surgery were passed around and numerous friends were shocked and awed at the pictures. They could hardly believe the size and ugliness of the layers of that dark cancer. We all knew God had granted another miracle of faithfulness and grace. Rick's life had been spared and there would be more dreams to dream and risks to take and more Kingdom work to be done in Jesus' name. (I would love to include a photo of the tumor so you could grasp the magnitude of it, but Rick might never forgive me!)

It would be a little while before I would recall the Scripture from Isaiah 58 that Beth had sent me some time before: "…then your light will break forth like the dawn, and your *healing* will quickly appear..." I am so glad I saved that email in my journal!! Confirmation! Rick's healing, through surgery, occurred quickly after learning of his cancer through the tenacious care of Dr. Webb. The fulfillment of that Scripture sent via email, before I even realized what it was really about or what it fully meant, was significant and miraculous. That passage was in neon lights and smack in my face. Thanks again, Beth, for sending that Scripture which was significant.

During Rick's time of recovery in the hospital, with friends surrounding his bed, Rick and I suddenly recalled in an epiphany moment the word spoken years ago that Georgette had given us after the lamb and mint jelly dinner in Canada. We shared it with those around Rick's bed. How had we forgotten for a time the important prophetic word she gave us years before? "God HAS to take you out of Canada to save your *life*, Rick." Only now did we realize the impact of those words. Dr. Webb had no idea other than obvious pneumonia what was going on in Rick's body. Rick's only other symptom in those years was the perpetual coughing and exhaustion. He had no pain in his kidney area. I honestly believe with my whole heart that had things been routinely going on as usual in Canada, his cancer would not have been found and dealt with before it was too late. Wow! It all made sense now. God somehow used a very few church elders to do the hard thing in order to allow God's perfect will to be done. And Georgette confirmed it to us long before we understood the hard plan that He was in control. Let the generations hear of God's faithfulness and rejoice!

If God tells you in your spirit to do or say something or if God gives you a word specifically, do not be afraid to let God use you to bless someone...or maybe even warn someone. Listen to God's voice! Sometimes what we do not understand in the present will be huge confirmation much later of what God is doing or preparing on your journey of life. It might be intended to confirm something in your own life or someone else's life. But be sure it is GOD making it clear to you and that it follows Scriptural teaching. It is not intended to accuse or divide or go against God's Word. Georgette's strange words didn't make any sense to us until years later. Because she specifically told us years before what she knew in her heart, it was God's confirmation many years later that He cared deeply for us! His thoughts are toward us all the time!

During Rick's recovery our daughter made a DVD album of digital photos for us of the entire process. They had special meaning, ending with photos of Dr. Webb taking out Rick's stitches across his abdomen. The long scar. Behind the photos played the music by Sara Groves again, "and in your hands...the pain and hurt look less like scars and more like character." Oh, yes, we cried again. Those lyrics I recalled meant even more to us now as we viewed the DVD! Thanks for the encouragement, Nikki, and this incredible song, Sara!

A few years later on October 22, 2008 Rick received a letter from Dr. David Christ. "I am pleased to report that your CT scan and chest x-ray show no evidence of any recurrent disease. I would recommend that you follow up with us in about six months again. The highest incidence of recurrent cancer is within the first three years of your initial surgery..." Again, Isaiah 58:8 comes to mind. "Your healing will quickly appear." Rick is cancer free to this day, and I still have those compelling photos to remind us of God's goodness. Rick would prefer hiding them where no one can find them! Rick is not one to ever look back, but only forward. This has always been amazing to me. He is a gift to me in so many ways. Psalm 27:13-14: "Yet I am confident that I will see the Lord's goodness while I am here in the land of the living. Wait patiently for the Lord. Be brave and courageous. Yes, wait patiently for the Lord."

I am singing the hymn again: "God works in mysterious ways, His wonders to perform...Ye fearful saints, fresh courage take; The clouds ye so much dread are big with mercy and shall break in blessings on your head...His purposes will ripen fast, unfolding every hour; the bud may have a bitter taste, but sweet will be the flower. Blind unbelief is sure to err and scan His work in vain; God is His own interpreter, and He will make it plain." (William Cowper) Cowper himself suffered a lifetime of deep sadness and extreme depression, even attempting to take his own life. Yet, he penned words full of God's mercy that would salve my soul as they presumably did his.

Zephaniah 3:17: "The Lord your God is with you, He is mighty to save. He will take great delight in you; he will quiet you with His love, He will rejoice over you with singing." Song of Solomon 2:12: "Flowers appear on the earth and the season of singing has come." Isaiah 62:4-5: "No longer will you be called deserted or name your land Desolate...Your land will be called Beulah for the Lord will take delight in You." God will rejoice over you.

Less than two weeks after Rick's surgery, our friend Dr. James Webb was prompted to write and send this poem to us on May 9, 2006:

RADICAL HEALING

(An Ode to Richard D. Porter's Nephrectomy)
The Great Physician's hands and feet

Enter His sacred bedside place.
Gaping wounds and broken hearts meet
Grace and mercy's full, warm embrace.

The hidden need, unknown desire
Are fully known and made aware.
Passion's cry ignites the fire—
Soothing balm flows from tender care.

Closure comes across the decades.
The scar sustained over time, fades
Before our very eyes.

That "dark thing" was not an obstacle to block our progress, make us doubt, or make us feel hopeless in the darkness. God was with us.

CHAPTER 24

Brokenness, Blessing and Mission

It's doubtful that God can bless a man greatly until He has hurt him deeply.

—*A. W. Tozer*

While I was watching TV one day, a woman spoke a word to my heart. "The glory of the present house will be greater than the glory of the former house, says the Lord Almighty. And in this place I will grant peace, declares the Lord. (Haggai 2:9) Don't struggle with your past because you are in a new season of blessing. Posture for it!" She spoke exactly what I needed to hear at that moment. Ready for that! Check!

Austrian holocaust survivor, Victor Frankl, acknowledged, "In some way suffering ceases to be suffering at the moment it finds a meaning." (*Man's Search for Meaning*) Our brokenness can be a prerequisite to God using us to care for others in loss or pain. Before we get too smug or proud of ourselves, remember God used a donkey at one time to verbally speak the word of the Lord to Balaam. (Numbers 22:21-39) Balaam was getting way ahead of God and an angel attempted to block his road to continue down a wrong path.

We learned through this season of our life that dead dreams and broken hearts are great preparation for helping others going through some kind of loss. A short time after our release from our church, our daughter Vonda and son-in-law Aaron were going through a "let go" from the church they helped plant and lead in Boise, Idaho. It came unexpectedly and a short time after they moved there specifically to help launch the church. We four being in the same place at the same time was crazy! We resonated with our Vonda and Aaron in their wounding. We hurt for them as parents. Unless one has gone through a wounding or loss or one has walked in those shoes, it is difficult to explain or empathize with the pain.

Our greatest brokenness may become our greatest ministry, even to the helping of others. We went through a time of suffering and grieving together. The fruit of brokenness can multiply in ministry beyond imagination. Not just because of wisdom gained or actions taken, but because of knowing and listening to God whispering how I can come alongside someone who may need me.

Our greatest problems can become stepping stones to greater spiritual strength. God promises He will not in any degree leave us helpless or forsaken, let us down or relax His hold on us. Hebrews 13:5b says, "Never will I leave you; never will I forsake you." Our faith grew. We were confident in God's faithfulness to us in our uncertain world, on an uncharted course, through an unknown future. God would turn our grievous circumstances around for His ultimate good. "Your days of sorrow will end." (Isaiah 60:20b)

Joel 2:25: "I will repay you for the years the locusts have eaten... the locust swarm...It was I who sent this great destroying army against you." God will restore what was taken from us as full compensation of what was lost in the past. He will make it up to us and we will have plenty and be satisfied. Praise the name of the Lord your God, Who has dealt wondrously with you. He is the God of restoration. He desires to restore to us as individuals that which Satan has stolen from us or that which we carelessly lost. Yet we must understand that everything belongs to God in the first place. (Haggai 2:8; Ephesians 1:3; Deuteronomy 8:18) God doesn't just restore monetary things. He restores His Word to the people. He restores holiness. He restores ministry of the gifts of the Spirit. He restores praise, worship and joy to individuals and the church. He restores families, relationships, health, joy, hope and faith in God, honor and zeal to serve God. "Forget about what's happened; don't keep going over old history. Be alert, be present. I'm about to do something brand new. It's bursting out! Don't you see it? There it is! I'm making a road through the desert, rivers in the badlands." (Isaiah 43:18-19, *MSG*)

As the great Danish theologian/philosopher Soren Kierkegaard put it, "Life can only be understood backwards; but it must be lived forwards." We could see so much more clearly down the road. Rick often reminded me, "You can't see the end of the parade from a beginning viewpoint on the curb. There is a bigger picture—a bigger landscape, a long parade, a tapestry in progress." God was perfecting His best plan for us all along. Humbling ourselves—that's what He wants. It can be turned into a badge of honor in the end. My small loss is part of a wonderful story, authored by God Himself. He was making all things new. I'm compelled to tell it!

No failure is fatal. I refuse to rummage through my trash heap any longer. I will go on. I choose to forgive.

One of our dear pastors on staff with us in a former church went through a deep hurt along with his wife. She would send emails of her deep sadness and helplessness. I was able to walk her through this time with emails of help, hope and prayer, to guide her through her process because we had walked the same road. A broken heart is great preparation to help another's hurt. This was one thing I had written to her in her pain out of my pain:

> Just accept that you are not in this situation alone or by chance. God has a plan for it all. And you lack nothing that His grace cannot give you as you pass through the fire. He will fulfill His purposes in you and you will come out stronger and better. Just hang in there and hang on to Him—He's strong enough to take ALL the weight of this. The soil of suffering will become the fertile ground for our seasons of fruitfulness again. These circumstances are beyond our understanding now, but God is closer than we know. God will not leave you stranded in any way. If He doesn't immediately calm the storm, He'll calm His child. We just believe some day that this will make sense, or it may not. But His glory will be revealed in us as we persevere through this. What God is

up to extends far beyond what the eye can see and the mind can imagine. There is an end to this ordeal.

God has brought quite a number of hurting pastors and spouses and ministry people into our lives lately because they have heard or know what we've been through. We have learned that God's people hurt God's anointed in horrible ways. Some stories are deeply disturbing. One couple shared that they were fired and asked to leave the church. The congregation gave them a turkey as a "get-away" gift. Incredible wounding and surprising insensitivity. We agonize, empathize and hurt with these couples and are able to listen to their story, pray them through the hard times and share our story of grace, forgiveness, restoration and reconciliation with them.

Michael W. Smith, on helping others, said, "Transformation in the world happens when people are healed and then start investing in other people." We need to be full of compassion for those who have been wounded, hurt, set aside, and discouraged. We may always walk with a limp and carry scars, but we will always sit at the King's table! As time goes on, our scars look more like character. He will always perfect that which concerns me. I can cast all my care upon Him because I know that He cares for me as I submit to Him. I can rejoice because I know that all things work together for good.

Years after our departure from Canada, now living in Iowa and moving beyond the past, I felt I was completely healed of the wounding and nagging questioning. It really didn't matter anymore. I figured it was about time to let my old journal "go" because it was filled anyway, many grievances released. Plus, I had a binder full of notes, quotes and emails that had been reviewed enough already! My mother-in-law, now in heaven along with Dad Porter, had given me a new journal years before and I thought it was timely to start fresh and new! It was a relief and joyous transition to the new journal. A fresh start! At the beginning of the new year.

I found journaling paid some rich returns as I pondered with paper and pen. It told the truth about my heart and feelings. It certainly wasn't polished. It helped to write out the worst of what I was feeling, all the crummy parts I hoped no one would ever find. Then it does the heart good to ask God for insight and truths and His Word...and journal some more of God's work inside of me. As C. S. Lewis said, "Whenever you are fed up with life, start writing: ink is the great cure for all human ills, as I have found out long ago."

CHAPTER 25

A New Day

Every morning starts a new page in your story. Make it a great one today.

—DOE ZANTAMATA

TODAY IS A new day. Take a deep breath and start again. Seize the wonder and uniqueness of today! Taste it! Recognize that throughout this beautiful day you have an inconceivable breadth and expanse of opportunities to catapult your life into what God has for you. With each new day comes new strength for every opportunity. "Each new day is a new beginning to place past failures behind and gained wisdom in front." (Owen Campbell, Jr.)

God's turnaround nature allows the hard places to become livable again. Every new day is a chance to allow God to change something in your life and to feel blessed for what you have. My expectation for God's good purposes was a hope of a new season in the physical and spiritual realm. Ezekiel 12:28 is a verse that popped up as I desired redemption in every area of my life: "This is what the Sovereign Lord says: 'None of my words will be delayed any longer; whatever I say will be fulfilled,' declares the Sovereign Lord." All delay has ended. God would do it *now*.

Another verse that God put in neon lights for me on January 1, 2008 at the beginning of the New Year was from Psalm 65:11 from the *New American Standard Bible*: "You crown the year with your goodness and your paths drip with abundance." It seemed the key words God was giving me were fertility and abundance for the coming year. I did not understand at the time about the fertility part. Maybe God meant He would not abort or miscarry His purposes or plans for us. I trusted there would be some semblance of fertility, victory and productivity in our lives on our journey with God in another new year—related to our job, family, or our lives in general. God's plan is always at work and I am part of that. One thing that fertility could also have meant was that our daughter-in-law had a miscarriage just before Christmas, their first baby. This verse from the Psalms was my first journal entry of 2008 in my brand new journal. (I desired that they, son Sean and wife Stacy, could bring forth a baby soon. Elijah was soon born, our 4th grandson. Then Addison came along. And then Declan). "You crown the year with your goodness and your paths drip with abundance!" I love it!

"Come on, let's go back to God. He hurt us, but He'll heal us. He hit us hard, but He'll put us right again. In a couple days we'll feel better. By the third day He'll have made us brand-new, alive and on our feet, fit to face Him. We're ready to study God, eager for God-knowledge. As sure as dawn breaks, so sure is His daily arrival. He comes as rain comes, as spring rain refreshing the ground." (Hosea 6:1-2, *MSG*)

My second entry in my new journal was the first Sunday of January, 2008. Rick was preaching from Numbers 10:29-11:23 in a church in Milford, Iowa. As I looked up the text in my Bible, I was struck by the fact that I had January 5, 2004 written by those very verses and that four years earlier to the very weekend Rick had preached that same text full of hope, faith, vision and passion to trust God in the New Year at the church in Canada. And a few days later, after preaching this text, he had been invited to resign—in part because "he lacked vision to lead the church." I could hardly focus on Rick's message that day because my mind was all over the place. How does God orchestrate these dates? Without that date written in my Bible, I would not have remembered that it was the very anniversary Sunday, four years previous, that Rick had preached the same text in our Abbotsford church. The same message of hope for the future! Rick rarely preaches "barrel" sermons unless I beg, but that message was meant for that day, the first Sunday of 2008. I really struggled that morning as I remembered.

February 11 friend Kathy Skalbeck gave me a poem she had written. She had been contemplating Abraham and Isaac's story and the ram that God provided in the thicket. She wondered how many times God had provided a ram in her life, sometimes at the last moment. (God had miraculously spared Kathy's life after a bicycle accident that left her near death. Enter Dr. Webb to save her life out in the middle of nowhere on a country road between Spirit Lake and Jackson, Minnesota. Members of our care group were biking together at the time of the accident. She was airlifted to a Sioux Falls hospital. A miracle of survival and healing, in the end, from the hand of God.) Then Kathy related to me about a women's conference she had attended over that past weekend where they had sung a song, "Held in His Rams" which was a typo for "Held in His Arms." Hmmm! God has a sense of humor. I love it. God, please hold me in your arms and continue to provide the rams in my life.

She composed this poem after thinking about the rams/arms typo at the retreat and sent it to me:

Jehovah Jireh,
I trust You
To provide the rams in my life.
The thickets are all around me—
So are Your rams.
With every ram
Comes a shofar.
Your provision complete.

Love ewe, Kathy
Held in His arms (rams).

Provision in the thicket!

Today is a new day. Take a deep breath and start again.

CHAPTER 26

Winter Wine

An anniversary says, "Think of the dreams you have weathered together. They are intimate accomplishments."

—Charles Swindoll, *Growing Strong in the Seasons of Life*

As Rick settled into his new job, we saw God's hand in everything. Rick continued to preach across all denominations. If I listed them all, it would be amazing to note the streams of traditions and persuasions. It is fascinating for me to accompany him to such diverse places. In addition, his responsibilities always include fundraising letters to write, a large amount of money to raise, counseling to do, office work that never ends and ministry on a daily basis. Of course his primary job is leading the annual Bible Conference at the beginning of August (okobojiconference.org).

Seven years to the very weekend of our release from our British Columbia church, (five years after moving to Iowa) Rick was asked to preach in a little white country church with a bell tower in a tiny town along a river nearly an hour south of our home. This was Rick's first invitation to this particular church in Linn Grove, Iowa, out between the corn fields. (I felt that day as though we were following in my grandfather Abraham Esau's footsteps as an itinerant preacher by horseback in the early days of the Christian and Missionary Alliance denomination. But we traveled by car, not horse!)

As we drove to the church that morning, we thought of anniversary dates, as we often did. Rick has an acute memory for anniversary dates, times, events, along with their import and significance. So often they had meaning and impact beyond our comprehension and it would take time to understand. We recalled as we traveled to church that it had been *seven* years to the very weekend of our release in Canada. Wow! The number seven is significant. The perfect number of completion. We speculated what God might do that day. I was tired and not terribly excited when we pulled up to the church building. Rick told me that it might be a long morning and suggested we make the best of it whatever it was.

After entering the church, friendly people greeted me. One could almost feel the kindness at the door. After a bit of pleasant conversation, I went to my usual seat of choice in the front. I remember Rick preached that day on Mephibosheth, crippled in both feet and rejected, but he sat at the King's table all the days of his life. Rick still has great ankle pain in both ankles/feet and swelling in the fused ankle. Countless numbers of people over the years have prayed for his healing. He gave the sermon illustration of his ankle issues. His message was well received and there were "Amens" from the congregation.

After the message a man went up to the platform and said he believed the people should gather around Rick and me to pray for our healing. He also said that they wanted to wash Rick's feet (as an example of servanthood and a sign of humility and blessing just as Jesus performed foot washing as recorded in John 13:14-17).

They knew nothing about our emotional hurt from seven years previous to that very weekend in Canada. They just felt led to pray for us. We gathered in a circle holding hands and thoughtful, sensitive people began praying for us. The words they prayed were directly related to the pain of our past and the pain of Rick's ankles. How did they know how or what to pray into our specific situation? I wept as they specifically prayed for us. I knew God was continuing to make Himself present and known to us, even on the seven-year anniversary. We both felt loved by people who knew nothing of our past and healing was continuing to wash over us even though I felt whole by this time. Maybe it was because we had just recalled the anniversary of seven years that God sent us a reminder that He was still with us on our journey. It was significant. It was God! It was a reminder of the time Rick washed the feet of Sevenoaks' elders near the end of our tenure in Canada. He felt led of God to do it. Now seven years later he received the washing.

There is more to the story. During our long "winter wait" time in Canada, we had visited one of many vineyards in the Okanagan area where we saw vats and cellar storage rooms and the wine store at the conclusion of our tour where all kinds of wines were for sale. Winter wine or ice wine had been explained to us on the tour. The grapes are not picked until after the first heavy frost and the grapes are slightly frozen. Ice wine is the sweetest wine and those wines in particular had been bottled the year before. However, waiting on the wine to age for a time would be beneficial, they told us.

It somehow seemed significant at that moment to purchase that wine and carry it with us, waiting until the time God would show us the exact healing moment to open and drink of the vine (crushed grapes) of healing and blessing. We had never in our life purchased a bottle of wine before that time. Yet, we both felt compelled to purchase the sweet ice wine as a metaphor for healing. We determined that we would not open that bottle of wine until we felt completely and totally whole in every way. Occasionally we would discuss together over the years, *when* is the time? It never seemed to be the right time, nor did I have a taste for wine anyway so what was the hurry? In reality I wasn't sure where the bottle had been stored since our move five years previous. (Remember we stayed in Canada two years after the church incident.) Though our pain seemed to be past, we had no closure on the meaning of the wine and frankly, it was not very important to us.

After an extended prayer time and foot washing on that seventh anniversary Sunday, we were invited to a couple's home for a wonderful Sunday meal. I did not realize initially that two other couples were invited as well. While we waited for dinner, a lady marched into the home with a "vivace" flair. Another musical term meaning lively, with spirit, vivacious! She and her husband had brought two bottles of wine to contribute to the dinner and the woman was animated and dramatic! Almost immediately I remembered *THE WINE*! The sign of completeness and wholeness! At seven years to the weekend with that kind of fanfare, how could I miss it? Seven years! NOW, right now, must be the time for the wine! The sign of completion of our healing!

I was struck by the woman's animation. She was excited because they had prepared and bottled this wine from their own vineyards. It took Rick longer to realize this was *the wine* and now was *the time* to celebrate complete healing, past be gone! I chuckled quietly at the pirouetting of the lady with the wine. She explained to us that they own vineyards on their property right down the road from where we sat, and made their own wine, one of them being sweet "winter wine" from slightly frozen grapes. She informed us that they ran a bed and breakfast on their property as well and purposed it for ministering the love of Jesus to those whom they served. We had seen a sign along the road to the *Innspiration B & B and Vineyards* as we approached the home for the dinner. As we saw the sign, we wondered if it was a Christian retreat center. Then we actually met the owners at the dinner!

Needless to say, we chose to drink the ice wine that day from a vineyard a few miles away and it somehow felt good! It felt like the very smile of God. As we raised our glasses, it was as if Christ Himself was raising His hands to deliver a toast with scars in His pierced hands. In blessing and healing! I deeply understood! Because of those scarred hands we are healed! To this day, we consider the moment a completion of the old and beginning of something new! New sweet winter wine! One church in one season had wounded us. Another church, in another place and season, had miraculously acted out healing, foot-washing, and then celebration without any knowledge that they were doing so on the seventh anniversary of the ecclesiastical train wreck. The wild realization was that we didn't even have to *supply* the wine as a sign of completion. God supplied it through this couple in His timing. I sensed a release in my spirit. *A completion*. An end! A beginning!

That day seemed significant in the Kingdom and in our lives. I had listened over and over to Brian Doerksen's song from his *Level Ground* album:

Will You Love Me in the Winter?

Changes bring a chill as the last leaves fall and the winter closes in.
I try to stay warm but it's hard alone In the dark night of my soul.
My heart aches, I feel numb, I struggle to go on
When my body breaks when my thoughts have failed
Will you love me still
Will you love me still in the winter
I remember spring, the thrill of budding life
Now just a faded memory
I gave what I could, did my best to serve
Now there's nothing left to give
My flesh fails my thoughts collide this question lingers
Will you love me still
Will you love me in the winter? (Used with permission—brian-doerksen.com)

I felt every word of those lyrics early in our journey. But winter was now in the past! The long winter was over!

Winter helps us by inviting us to do the inner work of the soul. However, living in attentive inactivity was not necessarily as inviting as I would have liked. I tried to remember the fragrance of the flowers… maybe even perusing garden seed catalogs of brilliant flowers for such a time as the coming spring. I love beautiful things! Yet Marcel Proust wrote, "We don't necessarily need new landscapes; we need new eyes."

A short time later I received a surprise gift from friend Dorita in Abbotsford that confirmed the end of our winter. She wrote a note to us and sent a CD by singer/songwriter/performer Cathy A J Hardy with two specific songs marked for me to listen to because she sensed they were specifically for me. Indeed they were—spiritually impactful. One of the songs from her *Love Shines* album was:

Winter is Over

"...the long winter is over, winter is past.
A new day dawns, at last hope for tomorrow.
An end of sorrow, beauty for ashes.
Springtime has come.
A blade of grass so tender yet so strong;
Your love so tender yet strong.
Your love has healed me;
Springtime has come...Sing, sing, sing!"
(Used with permission—cathyajhardy.com)

Yes! It did feel like the winter was over. It was long and cold. But the long winter was over! Springtime was singing!

"Look around you! *Winter* is over; the winter rains (snow, in our case) are gone! Spring flowers are in blossom all over. The whole world's a choir—and singing! Spring warblers are filling the forest with sweet arpeggios. Lilacs are exuberantly purple and perfumed and *cherry trees* fragrant with blossoms." (Song of Solomon 2:10-13, *TLB*) I love it! Cherry trees again!

Yes! Winter in the rearview mirror; singing has come. Cherry trees will soon produce again. The dance! Sweet! Healing complete! God is in control of the times and seasons. The dry seasons and winter are testing times. Thank God He is in control of the hard times and the desert seasons. "Though the fig tree does not bud and there are no grapes on the vines, though the olive crop fails and the fields produce no food, though there are no sheep in the pen and no cattle in the stalls, yet I will rejoice in the Lord, I will be joyful in God my Savior." (Habakkuk 3:17-18)

Psalm 4:7, KJV: "You have put gladness in my heart..." Joel 2:21: "Be glad now and rejoice! The Lord has done great things..." Nehemiah 12:27, NKJV: "Celebrate...with gladness, both with thanksgivings and singing."

CHAPTER 27

Not Abandoned

For the Lord will not abandon His people, nor will He forsake His inheritance.

—Ezekiel 39:28, NASB

One of the blessings of moving to Iowa was that I finally would be closer to my siblings and their families and my parents in Minnesota. I knew I needed to be near my parents in their golden years. I had been away from them most of my married life—too long.

It was not long after we returned to the Midwest that my dad was failing. His diabetes had compromised his kidneys to the point of them not functioning. He spent plenty of time in hospitals and clinics in three states to figure out what was causing some disturbing additional ailments. He had gone through surgery, severe reaction to meds, had pneumonia and congestive heart failure. It became clear when his kidneys failed that he would have to begin routine dialysis.

Mom (Carol Herman Esau) and Dad (Gilbert Donald Esau) lived in Mountain Lake, Minnesota all their married life and Dad all of his life. My grandfather, Abraham Cornelius Esau, born in 1886, immigrated to the United States from Wernersdorf, Molotschna Colonies, Ukraine (57 German Mennonite villages) with his family as a boy. My grandfather later married Grandma Helena Bargen Esau whose forefathers had also emigrated from a similar area of the Ukraine—then known as West Prussia. Grandpa's forefathers had relocated to numerous places in Europe and northern South America in search of religious freedom. After arriving in the States, horse-drawn covered wagon was the mode of transportation of the families of my grandparents who moved from place to place before finally settling in Minnesota where my father was born.

My dad served on the city council for nine years and then was elected Minnesota State Representative, serving for 18 years in state government. He served with six governors. Later he became mayor of Mountain Lake. After the age of 75, Dad traveled around the world with global lay evangelism (Church Partnership Evangelism out of Abbotsford, British Columbia of all places) on 16 or 17 different mission trips all over the world. We lost track because he visited so many countries. We have thousands of photos to attest to his travels. The many overseas mission trips were extremely important to him and he'd carry heavy bags of Bibles on foot up to mountain villages in extreme heat until his strength was nearly gone. No matter what the weather, how he felt physically, or how old he was. Countless people prayed to receive Christ on those trips.

Dad was in demand as a speaker all of his years. We were all so proud to attend his speeches as a family when we were able. He was especially in demand on Veteran's and Memorial Days. His patriotism, passion for his country, and his WWII stories captivated all who listened!

Dad had directed our church choir for 17 years and led congregational singing most of his life, often accompanying on trombone. Mom sang or played piano or organ. Daddy sang LOW bass in the Gospel Four Quartet that traveled for years! In later years he pastored two churches. He and Mom sang duets everywhere they went; Dad accompanied on the autoharp. He was an active, persevering man, an exemplary member of "the greatest generation." My appreciation for him grew across the years. He was surely not a perfect dad. But he was a good man and my parents' trajectory was toward Christlikeness across all of their years.

Now with his serving years past and with declining health and abilities, he needed a change. There were no dialysis clinics within an hour of where they lived. It became clear we would have to move my parents closer to dialysis since it would involve many hours in treatment, three days every week. My siblings and I determined the best place for him would be in our town, Spirit Lake, Iowa, with a dialysis center near our home.

I was working part time at Cherish House, a group home for unwed teen girls, and was teaching private piano lessons. We moved Mom and Dad into assisted living about three blocks from our home. I would take care of them as long as needed and could be flexible with my work for a while. I was so thankful that finally I was living near my parents and would not feel so much regret for having lived far away for so long. My desire was to serve them.

My routine for the next six months would be daily care of Mom and Dad. They no longer were driving. Advocating for them in every way became a big responsibility. Much of Dad's medical care and hospitalization was through Veterans Hospital in Sioux Falls, South Dakota, Windom, Minnesota and also the Vet's Clinic and the regional hospital in Spirit Lake. Mother had various appointments and care in Mankato, Minnesota, at Mayo Clinic in Rochester, Minnesota and in Spirit Lake. So our days were filled with travel and appointments, in-home nursing care, training for CPAP for apnea, oxygen tank use, fittings for a wheelchair, and three days each week in dialysis. Getting Dad in and out of the car was a long ordeal especially when he had to use a wheelchair. I advocated hours on the phone to get the needed help. We sought help from so many doctors, especially for a difficult digestive issue that was an unbearable indignity for my very private father. So many treatments and hospitals—until every option was exhausted. Our family agonized for Dad.

In spite of critical decline, Dad tried to keep a positive attitude. The nurses at the dialysis center loved him. He would entertain them with his WWII stories and often talk about his wonderful family, grandkids, and great grandkids. He would sing in his magnificent deep bass voice to overcome pain, frequently quoting the verse from II Corinthians 4:16 to his doctors, "Therefore we do not lose heart. Though outwardly we are wasting away, yet inwardly we are being renewed day by day." Doctors told Dad they were not sure how he endured such pain, severe insomnia, and other issues. He had deep faith and lived one day at a time, always hoping for a better day. He'd grieve his problems just a short while and then remind everyone how good he had it and how good God was to him and how wonderful his family was to him. After dialysis he would barely get outside and into my car before honestly declaring, "That was hell." But then he'd quickly add that he needed to celebrate getting through another dialysis by going out for a fish dinner, his favorite!

In fact, as he concluded his last dialysis, knowing he was hungry, we offered to pick up food. He asked Rick for a fish dinner. Rick delivered it and that proved to be his last meal before he entered the hospital.

I was honored to serve Mom and especially Dad since he seemed to be declining more rapidly than Mom at that time. God placed me here without a doubt for such a time as this. Moving them to our town was not initially on my radar, but it became a mutual blessing for us. It was part of God's plan. Without our move to Iowa, this would not have been possible and without our departure from Canada we would have never moved to Iowa.

Dad had written his memories of serving during WWII on yellow legal pads over a few years, also pecking out a few pages on an old typewriter. As he edged toward age 90, we kids and some of our cousins really encouraged him to compile his memories in a published book for the sake of the family. I took on the project of typing and editing his book. Our desires became reality in the publishing of *My World War II Memories* by Gilbert Esau. My author brother Terry finalized the manuscript for publication and contracted a publisher. We actually had to reprint three or four times because it sold so well. This great book recalls events and battlegrounds of more than four years during WWII in Alaska, the Aleutian Islands, and various places in Europe. Dad shared stories from the Battle of the Bulge and the exploits of his 81st Field Artillery Battalion, not the least of which was the liberation of Ohrdruf, the first German concentration camp of WWII.

At age 89 Dad had lost his health but not his determination. He recorded a CD playing his baritone (he also played trombone and other instruments) in all-dubbed four-part harmony. Who knew? The former quartet singer now became a brass quartet all by himself. Again, my brother Terry, a veteran of the composing/recording/producing industry, helped digitally record Dad's old favorite hymns he had played all his life. I accompanied on the piano, spontaneously transposing them for the B-flat instrument. He sometimes quipped that he would play at his own funeral and that, he did. Via that CD, he played songs of heaven as the crowd exited. Leave it to Gil Esau to accompany the celebration of his own welcome to heaven!

In his last days, Dad could only spend the day surviving, taking pills and going to doctor appointments, oxygen tank in tow. Even that was totally exhausting. I would invite my parents over for dinner when they were able. I loved making Dad's favorite foods and he continued to eat fairly well in spite of appearing as a skeleton at the end. It became too difficult for me to get Dad from his wheelchair into the car so many times a week. An automatic lift chair was used to place him into his dialysis chair. We used a local medical bus service because it had a hydraulic lift and clip for the wheelchair. He had fallen a couple times and his skin was so thin that he would bleed if he touched anything and large sores just would never heal. The assisted living center called 911 when dad went into a diabetic coma one night. His diabetes had been volatile for a few years. Amounts of insulin he took several times a day could not regulate his blood sugar. Nothing made sense with dad's blood sugar levels or ailments. He was a conundrum to all his physicians. They so wanted to help Dad. They really liked him.

Then the end began. One night, in the middle of the night, he fell and broke his hip. For some reason, the emergency room x-rays missed the very serious break. We all knew something was wrong. Dad persevered through the broken hip in dialysis (using a lift) until we knew something was not making sense. He had excruciating pain. The fracture was finally discovered after more x-rays. When dad heard the descriptions and saw exactly how bad the break really was, he knew it was the beginning of the end.

Dad's skilled nephrologist, who came every few weeks from Sioux Falls, South Dakota to the dialysis clinic to talk with me, called me and told me that no surgeon would risk the hip repair with Dad's major issues at his advanced age. Dad could no longer handle the pain of getting in and out of the dialysis chair or wheelchair or on/off the toilet. He was immediately hospitalized to care for the pain and my siblings and their entire families gathered around his hospital bed knowing that dialysis was no longer an option and that within days he would die.

The family gathered to sing to Dad, talk together in his lucid moments and enjoy the last days with him. He was not left alone any moment, even at night. His last phone call a few days before he died was from former Minnesota Governor Al Quie with whom he had served in state government. Dad was able to converse a few words with his friend Al. They shared that the next time they would see each other would be in heaven.

One of the precious memories of those days occurred while Dad was still lucid and engaged. His hospital room was packed with family. He began to speak blessings to his children, their spouses, and the families. He was especially tender toward the little ones. A pregnant granddaughter approached and he put his hand on her stomach, speaking a blessing over a great-grandchild he would not know here on earth. No dry eyes.

I brought a hymnal to the hospital and we all spent hours singing through the hymnbook with Dad. He had perfect pitch so he told us if we were pitched too high or low. Even then he would sing middle C for us to find our proper key! Everyone took turns sitting all night with Dad and Grandpa. He sang low bass as long as he could until his voice was silenced.

It was a Sunday evening and all family members had just gone home for Monday work. Rick was leading an annual outdoor area event, Praise in the Park, along West Lake Okoboji that Sunday evening. I was left alone with Dad at the hospital. I recalled that we had communion with him on one of his last good days and Scriptures were read. Rick, knowing that Dad was fighting for every breath by then as his lungs and body filled with fluid, read Psalm 16:8-11 the night before: "I will keep my eyes always on the Lord. With him at my right hand, I will not be shaken. Therefore my heart is glad and my tongue rejoices; my body also will rest secure, because you will ***not abandon*** (my emphasis) me to the grave, nor will you let your faithful one see decay. You have made known to me the path of life; you will fill me with joy in your presence, with eternal pleasure at your right hand."

Dad had not had anything to eat for several days and his lungs were filling with fluid that dialysis would normally take off. Toxins were oozing out of his arm pores. By Sunday evening he was fighting for every breath. I pushed the morphine every 15 minutes all night because I was in anguish over his fight to breathe. Just before dad became unconscious, I reminded him that I loved him. He responded with "I love you," which was spoken so clearly after struggling for a day to say anything. About an hour later he opened his eyes one last time and said to me, "Not abandoned." Those were his last words to me. I was amazed he had said those words, remembering the day before the words Rick had read from Psalm 16 to him. "Yes, Dad. God will *never abandon* us, not even in death." Even though flesh and heart fail. In these words of assurance is the confidence that, with God as Dad's refuge, even the grave could not rob him of life. "Not abandoned" were the last two words he affirmed back to me. I share them with you.

Mom joined me in the hospital because I knew Dad had maybe moments to live. Rick also joined us after his area-wide event. I sat by Dad's side until he took his last breath on July 16, 2012 at 6:06 a.m., a few short hours before our wedding anniversary. His celebration of life service was July 20, a few short hours before my birthday.

Any Scripture that says *not abandoned* is a tear jerker for me now. My daughter designed a pendant that says "NOT ABANDONED" on it and gave it to me for Christmas. Whether we are in a bad place in life, a loss, a failure, an illness, or a pain of any kind or description, we are reminded many times in the Scriptures that we are not abandoned! Not even in our deserts or pits or thickets or deserts or Maltas. Or in death. That has been a comfort for me as I remember our two years doing pit time and as I remember Dad's life and very last words.

"Because of your endless compassion you did *not abandon* me in the desert." (Nehemiah 9:19a, *GWT*) II Corinthians 4:8-9 in *The Message:*

"We are pressed on every side by troubles, but we are not crushed and broken. We are perplexed, but we don't give up and quit. We are hunted down, but God *never abandons* us. We get knocked down, but we get up again and keep going. Through suffering, these bodies of ours constantly share in the death of Jesus so that the life of Jesus may also be seen in our bodies."

In II Timothy 2:13 in the *Living Bible* we read: "Even when we are too weak to have any faith left, He remains faithful to us and will help us, for He cannot disown or abandon us who are a part of himself and He will always carry out His promises to us." Deuteronomy 31:6: "God is striding ahead of you. He's right there with you. He won't let you down; He will *not abandon* you and will never leave you or forsake you. Do not be afraid; do not be discouraged." I Samuel 12:22 "For the Lord will not abandon His people on account of His great name, because the Lord has been pleased to make you a people for Himself." You can do a word study on *not abandoned* or *not forsaken*. Here are a few more verses: Psalm 94:14; Psalm 37:25-28; Psalm 9:10; Deuteronomy 4:31 and 31:6 and 8; Joshua 1:5; I Chronicles 2:20; Genesis 28:15; I Kings 6:13; Isaiah 41:17; John 14:18; Ezra 9:9; Jeremiah 51:5; Nehemiah 9:17, 19, and 31; and Hebrews 13:5.

It was a joy to remember and honor a wonderful Godly father at his funeral. Sovereign God will someday wipe away all tears from our eyes. We are never abandoned! Not even in death!

CHAPTER 28

Reconciliation

Blessed are the peacemakers, for they shall be called the sons of God.

—*Matthew 5:9, ESV*

Remember "this is my (God's) doing" from the beginning of my journal from I Kings 12:24? I can let anyone who hurt me save face by saying, "You didn't do this to me; God did." Joseph told his brothers that God predestined that Abraham's descendants would live in Egypt. So God sent Joseph ahead of the rest of the family. Someone had to go first! God chose Joseph and he ended up preserving the entire family. I honestly do believe that "God HAD to take Rick out of Canada," as Georgette told us, "to save his life." We needed that realization to sink into our souls. Because the Joseph story and pit time resonated with us, we continued to relate to the story at the point where Joseph's brothers feared Joseph would take revenge. (Genesis 50:15-17) Joseph's assurance to his brothers in verses 19-21 was to not be afraid. God intended it for good, in the saving of many lives, which ultimately resulted in provision for their children in the years ahead. Joseph had forgiven them earlier and again later.

Rick always felt that someday, like Joseph who was always that metaphor for us, *if* his "brothers" would come back, he would need to accept them back, love and forgive them. To treat them as Joseph did his brothers. But nearly ten years had gone by since we left Canada. We felt completely healed of any past hurts and we felt no need for any kind of contact or reconciliation with our former church. We assumed with the amount of time that had passed, no contact would ever happen. We were truly OK with that. The bleeding had long stopped. There was a scar and a memory, but we had no need to live in the failures of the past whether enacted or received. God had already confirmed His plan in our lives and turned things around for good. Our journey continued with not just our hurt, but even our healing now in the rear-view mirror.

After our move to Iowa we had gone to a show on the life of Joseph in Branson, Missouri in the Sight and Sound Theater. What a moving presentation of the life of Joseph! We were captivated with every moment of the production. We felt like Joseph again, we resonated with the story, but we thought the fulfillment and restoration of the end of Joseph's life was far from what we would encounter or expect in our lifetime. Joseph had risen to a place of trust, leadership, and prosperity while serving in Pharaoh's court. Job had a similar experience. In Job 42:10 we read, "After Job prayed for his friends, the Lord made him prosperous again and gave him twice as much as he had before." It was OK if it didn't end that well for us. We were and are happy to be living a quiet season of God's faithful provision.

In the summer of 2012 the then pastor of the church from which we left contacted us by email. We only knew of him. Rick had briefly met him on a trip to Canada. His email indicated that the church felt led of God to begin communication regarding a process of reconciliation with us. He related that a man by the name of Genius Wells from Nassau, Bahamas had recently participated at our former church to speak at a funeral service. He shared at that time with the pastor and perhaps the elders that God would not bless their church until they made things right through a reconciliation process with former pastors. I do not know the circumstances of the way Mr. Wells warned them or if he claimed God had given this word of warning for them. In any case, it was from this insight that the pastor emailed us to inquire about exploring a process toward reconciliation. I had doubted there would ever be a point in time when we would actually sit down to discuss mutual grievances with anyone from our former church. Now I was encouraged by the inquiry and by Malachi 3:16 from *The Message*: "Then those whose lives honored God got together and talked it over. God saw what they were doing and listened in. A book was opened in God's presence and minutes were taken of the meeting, with the names of the God-fearers written down, all the names of those who honored God's name." We would take note of those who might be present to follow through with these "minutes of the meetings." Would there be resolution?

Malachi affirmed that there was a *time* and *place* where God's name was honored by specific people who sat down in an actual meeting to talk things over—and minutes of the meeting were recorded. It was a real event. With real people. With real dialogue. This heartened me. I understood that *forgiveness* was a change within myself. *Reconciliation* required a change within someone else. Reconciliation requires reciprocation or bilateral requirements on both sides to agree on the facts, the hurt, the motivation and that each can come to some understanding of the other's point of view. What is the compatible account of what happened, why it happened, and the consequences of what happened. In an ideal setting, it would require fact finding, truth telling, dialogue, empathy, fully telling our stories, acknowledging the pain and responsibility, apologies, and forgiveness for a meaningful transformation to take place. That's all-encompassing! II Corinthians 5:17-21 in *The Message* portrays reconciliation as a fresh start—old life gone, a new life burgeoning! "All this comes from the God who settled the relationship between us and Him, and then called us to settle our relationships with each other. God put the world square with Himself through the Messiah, giving the world a fresh start by offering forgiveness of sins. God has given us the task of telling everyone what He is doing. We're Christ's representatives. God uses us to persuade men and women to drop their differences and enter into God's work of making things right between them. We're speaking for Christ himself now: Become friends with God, He's already a friend with you. How, you say? In Christ, God put the wrong on Him who never did anything wrong, so we could be put right with God."

The Lord's Prayer shows our need for daily forgiveness as much as we need daily bread. It takes for granted that we need to be forgiven for our sins and that there are also people who have hurt, discredited, dishonored, been disloyal or lied about us who need to be forgiven as well. People fall short of respecting us or treating us with dignity. And we fall short in our handling of the grievances and in forgiving. So, this enquiry and invitation to open up communication toward reconciliation was a gift and it would need to go both ways—forgive our debts as we forgive our debtors.

Long spans of time passed between communications with our former church. It sometimes seemed unlikely that anything would actually happen to bring about a face-to-face meeting after all. It was during the time my mother was not doing well and I was very sick almost an entire year and in need of surgery, already scheduled during the middle of our communications. So, I knew that this invitation would not happen swiftly because I would need several months of recovery.

However, there came a time when an actual phone call came with the announcement of the choice of the mediator by the current elder board members who would lead us all through a process. After several email exchanges with Rick, it was concluded that the best mediator would be the very counselor who was such a help to us in the months after our dismissal. He already knew our story and our affection and respect for each other was mutual. What a blessing! We were only concerned that our prior relationship would cause the church to question his objectivity. On the contrary, they too had respect for his skilled mediation and trusted him to serve us all.

After spending hours on the phone with Dr. John Radford over several months, talking about the process and the possibilities of how it might come down, conference calls then ensued with the current board chairman and another board member, along with Dr. Radford, Rick and me. It seemed that the board did not want to specifically address any of our grievances which we submitted at their request. Our mediator didn't even want to tell us how they responded to the grievances *they* asked us to submit. Not a particularly encouraging beginning.

After the conference calls and prior to the face to face meeting, we narrowed our grievances down from a Letterman-like top ten to just two.

We did this in recognition that ten issues were just too many and clearly this board was not receptive to either the number or their content. We still felt ten grievances, but for their sake we would try to reconcile over two.

Recognizing that the current board chairman was not a part of the board when we were at the church, I assumed it to be difficult for him to engage the issues. I questioned the motivation of the request for reconciliation. Perhaps they were just looking for a face-saving easy way out. Was it because the church attendance was down and the large facilities were a financial burden that the smaller congregation could not maintain? I had heard that there was consideration to sell the building at one time. Was it because God's Spirit seemed to be more at a distance from that place and they wanted that sense of God's Presence and Spirit back? Was it because Genius Wells gave a prophetic word over a year prior to that? They felt some kind of guilt? Then we learned that the pastor who had followed us there and had initiated our communication months before had resigned to become the district superintendent. We wondered as to what that departure would do to the process.

More than a year after the initial contact for possible reconciliation by the church, we finally set a date for the church to fly us both up to British Columbia to engage in a process over a weekend (Friday and Saturday) and to leave open-ended decisions about what would take place on that Sunday during a worship service. There was talk of Rick preaching but he had argued for a two-part process, one for the hard work of reconciliation and the other for the celebration of the outcome if such was in order. In accepting a single trip, Rick did not feel comfortable promising a public statement of reconciliation with no awareness of how the private meetings would flow. Indeed, the non-response to our 10 grievances did not suggest that there would be a favorable conclusion.

The mediator even talked of inviting the entire community to a Sunday night event because of the fact that Rick had led the entire city in so many ways. Many from other churches might want to attend such an event as well as friends and former parishioners who now attended other churches. We were uncertain as to what to do. With many from our former congregation scattered and settled into different churches in the area, would anyone show up? Would our friends who had left when we left come back for the reconciliation? How would they even find out or learn about the weekend? I vacillated between feeling like this would be a miraculous revival with tons of people who I would love to see again showing up, and the whole weekend being a total dud.

As the time drew near for the reconciliation weekend and as I was recovering from a tough surgery, I knew I would need prayer support to follow through with this weekend. I had great fear, for some reason, that it may not go well and we would be hurt again. Could I be victimized again? Would I be able to venture out into life and feel protected from being injured again? I was actually panicking, which I realized was ridiculous and from the enemy. I knew God didn't bring us this far to leave us. Why was I filled with fear and dread?

I shared with my sister Brenda one morning that I was actually hyperventilating and was unable to function because I could not think clearly and could not process in my mind what the potential for good or bad outcomes might be. I shared with her that I didn't know what I'd say to the current elders, how much to say, how little to say...do I let the very few elders who were actually involved in our (ten years previous) grievances know how difficult they had made our lives? Only about three elders were common to both the original board and the current board. Only one member of the committee of three that encouraged Rick's resignation would be meeting with us. We were not sure then nor are we now as to whether that committee acted without board authority. Most of the individuals with whom we would meet would have no idea what happened in the first place. The truth was never clear from the get-go. And the elders involved ten years previously in our dismissal would not even be there. At least one was deceased. The former chairman of the elder board at the time we were there had left the church a few weeks before the appointed reconciliation weekend, so we were told. What did *that* mean? Why did he not want to engage in this? Why did he just leave the church as the reconciliation was scheduled? That was another one of those conundrums to me. Thoughts raced through my mind. Maybe I should say nothing in the meetings. Will we be blamed for something? Do they still have grievances with something Rick did or didn't do from ten years ago? What would be the godly thing for us to do? With this confusion in my mind, my sister prayed for me over the phone while I sobbed. Why would I feel this way if the church had reached out to us, wanting to make it as "right" to the degree they knew how?

A few friends in our town prayed for us and for the weekend. A couple even prayed in the aisle of the grocery store for God's covering over the weekend and for peace to cover us. I was growing some spine and strength! I miraculously gained total peace as I submitted it all to God, and was completely settled that God had it all under control. I felt ready to face this head-on. I felt God had rescued me from my fears. *Until* someone on Facebook wrote something on my wall that zapped the peace away from me so fast my head was spinning! It was so horrible that I assumed it was the devil uprooting and displacing my peace. But I seemed powerless to rebuke that post on Facebook. I was back at ground zero, if not worse than before. I pled with God to give back the peace that had been stolen from me. I felt violated. By one comment on Facebook!

After reading the devastating Facebook post, I sat sobbing on my living room couch. I felt like I had lost all the victory God had mercifully granted to me. Then the doorbell rang. I had no idea who was at my door and certainly didn't want to open it in my ugly pajamas with tears still streaming down my face. I was terrified it was someone I didn't know coming unannounced and that I could not explain my disheveled appearance. I had to make a split-second decision. The couch on which I was sitting was directly in front of the door. How could I escape? This could have been a fiasco but somehow I knew God works in mysterious ways His wonders to perform. He brings unexpected "angels" just when we need them!

I took a risk and opened the door in the middle of my mess. (That's when He *comes* to us—in the middle of our mess.)

Standing at the door, a lady who I knew at least by name said to me, "I'm not sure why I am here. God told me to come yesterday but I disobeyed and knew I had to come today." Oh my goodness! I knew this lady to be a prayer warrior who loved the Lord. I said to her, "I *know* why you are here!" And I think she relaxed a bit in the uncertainty of her risky reason to ring my doorbell.

I invited her to come in and to sit next to me on the couch as I cried out a specific reason God sent her to my door at that very moment. I told her, between sobs, why I was struggling about the peace and joy that had just been pilfered from me in one crazy post on Facebook. She spoke reason to me, exposed the evil force that it was, and told me I should not give so much power to one individual on Facebook who knew absolutely nothing of my situation. She spoke the voice of truth to me. She had even brought two books along to share with me. Only God could have sent her my way at the very moment I needed the truth perspective and sense spoken back to me. She laid her hand on my back and prayed for God's power and peace to return to me in a mighty way. She knew exactly what I needed to hear from a merciful God who loved me very much. Miraculous and instantaneous peace returned to my soul! From that moment on, throughout the entire process, God's Spirit rested on me with unexplainable confidence and shalom. I never looked back. I was ready for whatever was to happen. Truly a miracle from God!

God's Spirit told this lady to come to my door at exactly the very moment I needed truth spoken to me—what I already knew about God, but somehow had lost perspective permitting doubts to creep into my mind. I knew without a doubt that God had sent her. In retrospect, it just blows my mind how faithful God is to remind us **He** is the one that brings peace and help when we need it. I know how loved I am by the Father to grant me such grace. Anne, from the bottom of my heart, thank you for listening to God's voice and coming alongside me that day. Even if you thought it was a day late. God knew the timing and held you a few more hours for the moment I *really* needed your word from God. From that moment going forward I had complete perfect peace because my mind was stayed on Him. I knew God would not abandon me.

My sister sent daily cards in the mail with Scripture verses and prayers on them. I quit developing scenarios in my mind of what to say during our reconciliation meetings and rather simply trusted God to speak through me whatever He wanted at whatever time. No need to prepare any lofty words or arguments. Aaron and Hur were holding up our arms. (Exodus 17:12) Rick is generally not the nut case that I am and he alternated from being a bit unsettled and being at peace with whatever the process would bring.

Our youngest daughter wanted to fly up to British Columbia with us because she felt the violation and hurt as well and could not say her good-byes to any of her friends at that time. It seemed so sudden and bizarre to her as well. But the arrangements with her work and family just didn't allow her to travel with us. We didn't know if any of her friends were still in the church anyway after ten years. Most were likely married and gone.

The reconciliation weekend approached—October 25-27, 2013. We drove from our home in Iowa to the Omaha, Nebraska airport, flew to Seattle with a layover in Portland, rented a car and drove north to Abbotsford, British Columbia. A long day of travel. We arrived in enough time to drop our suitcases at our host home. The mediator then came to meet with us there in preparation for the evening session with the elders of Sevenoaks. He informed us, from his experience, what we could expect—really a gamut of scenarios that could not be predicted at that point. We were ready for anything. Without any time to pull ourselves together after long travel, we drove to the church for our first meetings.

I wouldn't say the greetings upon our arrival were happy hugs or any high-five-howdys, but the welcome to a painful place was amicable and polite. It was interesting to hastily scan the room to identify those with whom we would spend the next few days. Who would be there to share this intense time? Who wouldn't?

The mediator led effectively. He told us privately that at the end of the first evening of meetings, we might feel we had regressed to a point of no return. The possibilities ranged from breakthrough to total collapse of the process. We were prepared for anything at that point.

Our mediator, Dr. Radford was correct. It seemed we were getting nowhere. The real issues, including our abridged top two grievances, were brushed under the carpet. We didn't express our feelings...they didn't acknowledge the grievances we had submitted at their request or even ask questions of us. The subject of one of our two remaining grievances was marginally broached and it regarded me (the wife of the pastor—yet I was not employed in any way by the church). One elder admitted some culpability but didn't change his opinion or apologize. So I sat there and cried—the *only* time I cried that weekend. Interestingly, our mediator immediately jumped to my defense and I felt at peace. The tears were short-lived. The comment did not go any farther. The elder could have his opinion of me and I was OK with that and could let it go.

We had little opportunity to share the story of life since our days at the church. I was frustrated. I wanted to but was not given an opportunity. It all happened differently than I had imagined. Yet I knew God was in control and He knew what needed to occur and it wasn't up to me to force anything. I think I did mention Rick's cancer in passing. I wanted them to know that Rick had cancer in our last years of ministry in Canada but we didn't know it at the time. I was measured and controlled with my words when I was tempted to inject my "yeah, buts." There were moments when I felt we were wasting time.

One other former elder did take a stand at one point late on that Friday evening. He offered his opinion that the board did desire our departure from that pastoral ministry, though the board had always indicated that to them Rick's resignation was a surprise. In other words, he suggested that there had been duplicity. Five seconds of truth-telling was good! That was the extent of that. It was late and things were feeling impossible and no one picked up on this glimmer of truth.

The next day, Saturday, October 26, provided something of a breakthrough by afternoon. Dr. Radford asked Rick and one of the board members who served at the time of our departure to engage a communications technique. This was intended to help us all get in touch with issues, events, and feelings from ten years previous. To do so, he produced large foam building blocks of many shapes, sizes, and colors. Rick and the elder were instructed to choose and use the blocks to build a picture of all that was happening and all that they felt in those years. We had done this exercise at Oasis Retreat and Rick found it easy to tell our story in this way.

After a time of "building" and expressing through the blocks activity, Rick did something which we were later told changed the tone of the meeting. After a time in which both parties, Rick and the elder, chose their shapes and colors to tell their story, Rick picked up his biggest, darkest block representing his worst feelings and handed it to the elder. This, after the elder had shared deeply of his own great losses and struggles. Rick was in essence saying, "Your pain is of far more consequence than mine. There is only one block that expresses that. I will let you use it." Meanwhile, Rick grabbed two blocks, black and blue, and laughingly said he would let them represent our bruises. The man broke down and cried as Rick relinquished the biggest block to him.

At the end of the activity this man expressed more of his heart toward us and likely felt some of our pain over the last years as well as remembering and releasing his own terrible pain. Rick and I went over to embrace in a three-way-hug for a long while as the man cried. We didn't feel much of anything coming from any other board members in the room, not to say they weren't inwardly processing the moment.

Yet if this one man represented them all, it was OK. It was noble and good. The balm of a supportive embrace felt as though our wounded spirits were collectively comforting one another, if not to some degree healing us on the inside and I hope healing that elder as well. The other elders expressed very little in the entire process. So to this day I have no idea how the others were handling this reconciliation thing.

We discussed what would happen the next morning in the worship service. Dr. Radford reminded the board what their original intent for a Sunday reconciliation service was and what should take place. I remember thinking that I wanted to speak a positive prophetic word over the elders and the church before the meeting ended, but I hadn't spoken much at all and I was not going to imply that I needed the last word. I felt we needed to pray a prayer of forgiveness and humility and acceptance and love. Were we not even going to pray to cement our mutual forgiveness? It was ending too abruptly and with so little resolution. I had little opportunity to express all that I felt. Was this all that there would be after the commitment of so many to the risk and hard work of exploring painful old scars? Were my expectations too grandiose? I felt deflated and disappointed.

Years ago I "put away" a letter I had painstakingly formulated to tell the elders exactly how I felt. I wished I could someday share it with them. That was released long ago and those feelings had faded. But I yet had something on my heart to share before the reconciliation meetings came to a close. It was something quite different from my original letter. Some of what I now wanted to share was written down and some of it was the Scripture that Beth had emailed me as we had moved to Spirit Lake. Remember the Isaiah 58:8-12 passage? I felt that I wanted God to bless the elders and the church for requesting our presence for a reconciliation weekend regardless of how I felt the meetings had concluded. And to make sure they understood that all was forgiven and under the blood of Jesus and the grace of God and life would go on with renewed victory. It seemed the opportunity would not arise for me to share. The meeting seemed flat though our mediator did a great job of leading us in the process, doing his best to confront and resolve the issues. I only have positive affirmation for him. He had done his homework and there comes a point where you cannot force an outcome. We love you Dr. John Radford!

The immediate former pastor of the church, now the district superintendent, and his wife had been at the last Saturday meeting. It was good to have them in attendance. He was the pastor who started the ball rolling toward this reconciliation eighteen months before. We felt affirmation from them in spite of their lack of awareness of the past events. We appreciated their desire for the church to make things right.

Just then, toward the end of the last meeting, the mediator looked at me and said, "I believe Dianne has something to share and following that the district superintendent will close in prayer." Wow! I was ready! Armed with the grace and boldness of God, I was totally sure of the words He wanted me to speak out loud over the elders and the church. It was simple and short. But it was from God through my heart. I ended with these words from Isaiah 58:8-12: "...then your light will break forth like the dawn, and your healing will quickly appear (these words were previously for Rick and healing of his cancer, but now appropriated to Sevenoaks Church as well); then your righteousness will go before you, and the glory of the Lord will be your rear guard. Then you will call, and the Lord will answer; you will cry for help, and He will say: Here am I. If you do away with the yoke of oppression, with the pointing finger and malicious talk, and if you spend yourselves in behalf of the hungry and satisfy the needs of the oppressed, then your light will rise in the darkness, and your night will become like the noonday. The Lord will guide you always; He will satisfy your needs in a sun-scorched land and will strengthen your frame. You will be like a well-watered garden, like a spring whose waters never fail. Your people will rebuild the ancient ruins and will raise up the age-old foundations; you will be called Repairer of Broken Walls, Restorer of Streets with dwellings and your lives will turn around at once. Your righteousness will pave your way. The God of glory will secure your passage. Then when you pray, God will answer. You'll call out for help and I'll say, Here I am."

I asked God to open my heart and mouth and to honor His Word. He did that. "So is my word that goes out from my mouth: It will not return to me empty, but will accomplish what I desire and achieve the purpose for which I sent it." (Isaiah 55:11) God will bring these words to fruition even in the life of Sevenoaks Church.

The church had been tried by fire and through decline. I do believe, however, as Swindoll puts it: "Nothing can ever destroy the Church. It's a permanent building process that will never be crippled by some outside force, never be rendered obsolete, and never be stopped by any power, person, or plan."

True, the income wasn't there to support what the church once was. There were issues. (Aren't there *always* issues)? The current elder chairman acknowledged that the word I had given them at the end of the meeting indeed was a word from God for them and for the church in going forward. I was pleased God granted my desire to share with the elders a positive word of encouragement. We chose to release all else which was unsaid.

The last request was for Rick to speak Sunday morning at the reconciliation service. He had planned all along not to speak. By this time it was Saturday evening and we had a few events planned for dinner and into the evening with friends. Rick knew God would give him the words to boldly speak to the body of Christ at Sevenoaks for the next morning. God had not brought us this far to leave us now!

After an exhausting day of meetings and a late evening of blessings with friends, Rick decided to go to bed and get up early Sunday to jot a few thoughts down on a tiny sticky note. Yes, Rick could do this. He was great at sharing an appropriate word from the Lord on the spur of the moment. And the Spirit bore witness with Rick's spirit in applying prophetic and relevant truth.

Reconciliation Sunday came, October 27, 2013. Another grace de Dieu! We met long-time friends, Reg and Donna Reimer, for coffee at a local shop before the morning service. During our visit Reg gifted Rick with a beautiful carved wooden cross from Vietnam, placing it in Rick's hand. They had been missionaries there a long time and still made trips to advocate for the suffering, marginalized, persecuted Christians there. Reg often gifted us with unusual artisan gifts from his travels in Vietnam.

Then we rushed to church. Some of our friends who had left the church, having heard we were in town, came back for the service. We met in a side room with the elders and then walked in to the sanctuary the last minute as the service was about to begin. There were hand clasps and huge smiles and waves coming from the pews and across the aisles. The first half of the service was dull and nondescript. Our names were not mentioned in the service, nor were our names printed anywhere in the worship folder, nor was the reconciliation component mentioned until about 28 minutes into the service.

To be very honest, after almost 30 agonizing minutes, I wondered why we were there. I desperately wanted to get up and walk out. I had been patient long enough! I thought it was just plain weird. In the defense of those who planned the service, they couldn't print what they did not know. Rick had told them before the meetings that we could not promise our participation on Sunday if we felt the meetings did not go well. We did not desire to stand in front of the congregation and pretend if resolution did not occur.

Finally the elder board chairman got up and introduced us. Rick and I were invited to sit in chairs on the platform. All the current elders and the very few former elders who still attended the church came up to the platform, standing in a line behind us. The current chairman of the elders told of his growth in Christ under Rick's ministry in the past. He spoke of "broken" events and that things had ended raggedly as we left the church. He told of a complete stranger, Genius Wells from Nassau, who warned them of their need to reconcile when he visited to speak at a funeral back in March of 2012.

Dr. John Radford then got up and explained what was happening and how the service would continue. He informed the congregation regarding reasons to reconcile, what reconciliation is, and why we don't often follow through with it. He went through informative steps that needed to be followed for God to be honored. He admitted that forgiveness is not always complete because parts are missing and people involved are no longer around due to death or leaving the church. Both parts, true.

Dr. Radford expressed *for* the elders what they intended. And what God desires in contrition, repentance and forgiveness. He told of our meetings Friday and Saturday. Following this another elder who had been on the board for 9 of the last 11 years was invited to share his written statement—the same man who had done the building blocks exercise with Rick and whom we had embraced the previous day. I am not sure if he himself had written the statement that he read or if the elders participated in that report. It seemed it was his personal account. Other elders were invited to make a statement or share something but no one offered.

Really? Uncomfortable silence ensued. Rick looked at the elder chair and with a nod he invited Rick to the pulpit to break the silence. Another of Rick's gifts.

Rick spoke with freedom from the Gospel of John chapter 11, the story of Lazarus and his resuscitation from the dead. First, he thanked three older pastors who were present who had served before him and with him in the city, calling them "generals in the Lord's army" and blessing them and their spouses for their faithful service and partnership in the Gospel. He then spoke briefly of our meetings on Friday and Saturday and spoke release of any offense perceived or real, corporate or individual. I don't think that Rick ever referred to his little yellow sticky note.

From the Lazarus story he shared that opening an old grave was not a simple process. There was much risk in the trembling expectation that Jesus could make the dead live. The argument against opening the tomb was that Lazarus had been dead too long and that decomposition was too far advanced for recovery. Moreover the whole process would be offensive to the nostrils. But Jesus wanted to give life so the risk was worth it for the resurrection outcome. All the while Rick paralleled our story with Lazarus. However, God's glory would win; the word of life trumps the stench of death every time. Opening the door on death was a huge risk. The stone had to be rolled away.

When Lazarus *came out* of the tomb he was still wearing the garb of death, his faceless visage yet unrecognizable. Jesus said to unbind him and let him go. Rick's message to the church paralleled our story—unbind what was dead. Then let the dance of life begin!

Rick also blessed the Bahamian visitor, Genius Wells, for taking the risk of prophesying the need for reconciliation. He also mentioned former Pastor Errol Rempel who encouraged the reconciliation process and opened the door to it. These were both men who "rolled away the stone," risking the stench in expectation that reconciliation could equal resurrection for the Church, for relationships, and for the departed pastor and wife.

Rick also publically asked forgiveness from the church and the elders for his part in any alienation and ill-feeling that occurred. Without presumption of guilt on the part of the elders or the church, he nevertheless spoke forgiveness on behalf of himself and me over any hurts visited on us by the church. We had both desired a more specific reconciliation. It was clear that the best that could occur was a general reconciliation in full-as-possible trust that God Himself would be honored. The underlying hope was that both parties would be freed to continue to serve in confidence of His full blessing.

After Rick had spoken over the congregation what God had revealed for him to say which I felt was God-breathed and powerful, he walked down to the floor of the worship center. He then asked the congregation to stand if they wanted to visibly express their support for the leaders of the church. The elders had confided earlier that the church body didn't seem to trust them in recent times. Previous untruths, or at least withholding some truth, and the resulting confusion likely contributed to this. Admittedly I am not aware of all the reasons. Most people stood at Rick's invitation. As Rick, with raised arms over the elders, prayed for them and faced them as they stood on the platform, I stood with Rick with my arms raised over the elders as well, praying for anointing and life. Then we turned toward the congregation with arms raised to pray. I knelt. Some people were crying. We felt strong in the Lord and in the power of His might. We did the right thing.

After church long lines of people wanted to greet us and we didn't get past the front of the platform for a long time. I lost track of time. Beth, the lady who had emailed the Isaiah passage to me years before, pinned a corsage of three roses on me. She also gave me a card explaining the significance of the roses and their colors in light of the weekend. It was a thoughtful, meaningful gesture of love.

Dear friends, Mel and Carol Davis, whose son was dying of ALS, finally came up to us after a long patient wait. Most of the people in church had gone home. They asked if we could please go see their son and his young family to pray healing for him once more. Many had prayed for him. He was a gifted musician. We had prayed from a distance for Steve ever since we learned he could no longer play guitar because something was terribly wrong. His parents and their two young adult children had been so supportive of Rick and me during our years at the church. Steve, now stricken with ALS, had enjoyed Rick's ministry in the years we served the church. He would sometimes participate on the worship team playing his guitar and he had toured with a Christian band. Steve's wife, Karessa, had served on our church office staff while we were there and before they were married.

So we followed the Davis family to their son's home to pray healing for Steve. He was wheelchair bound and mostly bedridden at that point and barring a miracle from God, would not live much longer. Rick reached in his pocket and found the carved wooden cross that our missionary friend had given Rick at the coffee shop before church just a few hours before. Vietnamese artisans had prayed over that cross as they carved it, envisioning, by faith a blessing to the future recipient. It seemed right to place the cross in Steve's hand, kneel down at the foot of his wheelchair and contend with God for his life and healing one more time. There were lots of tears. Rick anointed him with oil as we begged God for a miracle. In God's Sovereignty, He took Steve home to heaven a short time later. He left behind a beautiful wife and two small children. How I agonize to this day with this wonderful family in their unspeakable loss. We love you Davis family.

Then we rushed over to Abbotsford Regional Hospital to greet and pray for Agnes Doerksen, Brian's mom, who was in serious condition and nearing the end of this life. We hated to awaken her, but she beamed when she realized we were there. She had been our prayer warrior for so many years and now it was our great privilege to pray for her, knowing her transition to heaven would be soon. God would never abandon her, not even in death. Rick read Scripture and we prayed for dear Agnes, a warrior in the faith. She radiated the love of Jesus even from her hospital bed.

As we were about to leave the hospital room and say goodbye to Agnes for the last time on this side of heaven, a woman walked in who we assumed was there to visit Agnes as well. Suddenly I realized I was looking into the eyes of the very physician who years earlier gently touched me as I released a flood of tears when she told me, "On behalf of anyone at Sevenoaks who hurt you, would you please forgive us?" It was not appropriate to scream in recognition at that moment. So we enthusiastically embraced and Rick captured that moment on my camera. Dr. Campbell and me! A coincidence? I don't think so! One short, incredible point in time. So weighted with the Grace de Dieu!

Dr. Milena Campbell was the *beginning* of my healing and with the reconciliation service now history moments before, God allowed the miracle of Dr. Campbell to show up again as the *end-cap* of my healing! She provided *book-ends* to my story. Oh, God is good! What a sacred moment.

Would I say that our reconciliation experience was all we hoped it would be? No! In fact it felt like we gave more than they gave. I do not remember a single elder praying for us or any elder personally or specifically asking for forgiveness other than in the Sunday morning public statement by one man. Maybe the whole process was more for *them* than it was for *us*. We can assuredly say that we love Sevenoaks Church and want God's blessing to be upon them and their ministry in that beloved city. We desire that God prospers them in ways they cannot even comprehend. After all, ten years of God's call and Spirit work in that place can seed Kingdom efforts with ripple effects for years to come.

Maybe the reason real forgiveness is so difficult is that the process is not all that neat and tidy. Forgiveness isn't an *event* but rather a *process* I choose to continue. I was surprised to read that C. S. Lewis admitted that only on his deathbed did he finally feel free of the last trace of anger toward his personal tutor in preparatory school, who had shamed him unrelentingly. Sandra Wilson's admission in *Into Abba's Arms* amused me: "I have discovered that forgiving can be a lot like packaging an octopus. Just about the time you think you have it all wrapped up, something else pops out!"

God expects forgiven people to forgive as affirmed in Matthew 18:21-35. Reconciliation is focused on restoring broken relationships. And where trust is deeply broken, restoration is a process and sometimes a lengthy one. It is not that easy to restore a broken relationship when there is no clarity from the offender about his/her level of repentance. It felt like their avoidance of issues or admitting any culpability meant they weren't really sincere or trying to understand our pain. However, the weekend event *happened* at their invitation, they desired to make it right to whatever degree it happened, and that is significant. It is all under the shed blood of Jesus. I worked through enough of the hurt by that reconciliation Sunday that I could say I no longer look to the ones who hurt me to make it up to me. I released them from having to make me OK. I can make the decision to look to God to make things right in my life. I needed this experience for God to show me how little it is about *me* and how much it is about *Him*. How I need not worry or fret about what to say in situations. God will say it through me as I release my concerns and needs, and listen to His voice. How well He knows and understands me and desires good for me.

I needed this experience to demonstrate to me that I should not try to hurry God to work His purposes in me. He may not release me from the pit until I have learned the reasons for His allowing me pit time in the first place. Or trying to figure out what God is doing when my world seems to be falling apart. Or to help me know that my *big* deal is *not* that big of a deal in the scope of things. A mere blip, hardly perceptible, on the map of the journey—the timeline of my life. I can look back on that super-charged, high-powered, up-tight time in my life and recall it as only a small issue, water under the bridge. God is always carrying me and will never abandon me.

All things seem to work out in the end. I pray it is all for God's glory. It gave me the quiet confidence that God is in control without a need to always understand the why or the what. Plus, my husband's cancer was miraculously discovered and his life was spared. We still trudge onward in the journey together. *Still Proceeding* with the One who bears the scars in His hands, carrying us when our journey is difficult!

Living hope is when we know that what happens here is ultimately leading us to our eternal home. It is the belief in the impossible. Our hope in Christ stabilizes us in our hurts and storms. Accept the mystery of hardship. Don't try to understand or explain every detail. Then deliberately trust God to protect you in His power and plan. (notes from Charles Swindoll)

It is great to feel there is dolce (musical term meaning "sweet") sonorous harmony resonating again in the music of my life. The echo will have ripples, waves and currents extending forward. To reconcile is to make right or harmonize! Reconciliation involved different parties coming to the same position, involving change, resulting in harmony again.

A wonderful post script to this chapter is that I have heard from a number of sources that God is blessing Sevenoaks Alliance Church in Abbotsford, British Columbia in greater measure since the reconciliation weekend. That has been my prayer and heart's desire for them. May God continue to grant restoration to the community of beloved believers in that city. May they be like a well-watered garden. The foundation remain strong. God bless them and keep them and make His face to shine upon them. Righteousness will pave their way and the God of glory and His Spirit will reign and rain in that place. Let the generations hear and rejoice!

CHAPTER 29

Life Goes On—Today

In three words I can sum up everything I have learned about life: it goes on.

—Robert Frost

Those three words, life goes on, make for a simple sentence but a complex process. The world doesn't stop for an injustice, a deep wounding, abandonment, pain, loss of any kind, an illness, terrorism, broken relationships, persecution, war, or death. Give it any name. Sometimes we feel life *should* just stop when our world falls apart. Our life can feel like it comes to a complete standstill because of a struggle. Yet others around us generally don't stop long enough to notice. Oh, our truest friends do for a time. There's so much to fix in this world that we become numb to what just ultimately gets endured in the depth of sadness or apathy. We cannot fix the world, but we can make a little difference one step, one person at a time. But if we mercy-give until it hurts or drains us of our strength, we may eventually need help ourselves.

As soon as my dad passed, (at about the time we were first being contacted by Sevenoaks Church) we were immediately thrust into the next issues—caring for my mom who had broken her wrist in a fall in early August 2012, just weeks after Dad's death. We had a bed for her in our home so she would not be alone after Dad died and she could attend the Bible Conference that she loved and attended all her married life. After her fall, a long titanium plate and nine screws were inserted in her right arm. Being unable to do much of anything for herself, Mom remained in our home to stay for a while so I could care for her. We expected Mom to rally and get stronger after Dad died, but every day became a struggle for her with more compounding issues.

We moved her into assisted living in The Lodge in Mountain Lake, Minnesota. It proved to be too difficult with her health issues to maintain her home of 66 years. Over time we kids went through a lifetime of stuff, all of her earthly belongings. In July 2013 we sold almost everything in an auction. Mom then rented her home to our youngest daughter Nikki and family who moved from suburban Minneapolis to Mountain Lake in mid-August. Nikki's husband Aaron had taken a job as full-time music teacher at Mountain Lake Christian School. Living in Grandma's house would be perfect for them. Rick and I helped them do some renewing and improvements in Mom's home. The Christian School was the same school my Dad had attended, I attended and then I became the very first full-time music teacher there. Three of Dad's great grandsons (my grandsons), Timothy, Samuel and Ezra are now in the same Mountain Lake Christian School. Another slice of interesting heritage and another grace of God. Nikki and Aaron have a music ministry called House of Aaron. Check them out on Facebook—House of Aaron Music.

After moving to the assisted living facility, Mom had a stroke in early April of 2014 resulting in paralysis on her left side. After a hospital stay we moved her to the Good Samaritan Village nursing home in Mountain Lake. She was on a feeding tube, unable to swallow. She had intense herniated disk back pain, macular degeneration, congestive heart failure, and was on medications for muscle spasms due to paralysis, seizures and pain. We believe other strokes followed. It was hard to watch mom go downhill for a year and four months with almost no communication and little engagement. I grieved as I sat by her bedside during those long months. She entered her permanent home in heaven July 20, 2015. My desire was always to come back to the home of my youth for these days. God granted my request. What a blessing! This was part of God's plan.

Several years ago before Dad took his downhill turn our daughter Vonda, husband Aaron and son Timothy moved from Boise, Idaho to live with us for some months while looking for work and a home in Southwest Minnesota. They remodeled a lovely home they purchased in Mountain Lake and both found jobs. It is such a joy to have both daughters and families closer to us now. Both in my home town! Who would have thought it?

The rare times we fly out to Junction City, Oregon to see our son Sean and his wife Stacy and family (Elijah, Addison and Declan) are delightful times of reconnecting with our far-away family. We miss them a lot.

Our daughter Nikki's cancer surgery and radiation is in the past. We trust that God is working His purposes in her. Life goes on.

CHAPTER 30

Final Thoughts

God can take my past and make it work together for my good – so brilliantly and beautifully that I will be tempted to say, "That is the way it was supposed to be!"

—*Dianne Porter*

I look back on the last few years and wonder how I survived. Yet God has always been faithful. In the middle of all this I experienced a year-long illness myself, constant pneumonia followed by surgery for gastro-esophageal reflux disease on March 15, 2013. I have recovered well. That followed with three eye surgeries over five months. God has been faithful throughout the journey and I know He isn't finished with me yet. I continue to trust Him for his touch in my life. I'm climbing out of the rubble... and the scars look more like character.

Our battered armor and scars solidify our overcoming victory. We overcome through the blood of the Lamb and the word of our testimony. We sit at the King's table every day of our lives, and there are always baskets of leftovers!

The notion was in me that I should always get along with everybody, be liked by everybody, and that conflicts between Christian people should not occur. I felt this, especially as a pastor's wife. I do not like conflict. It unsettles me immensely. I attempt to return kindness for heartlessness. Yet, not even God's early servants, Paul and Barnabas, could work together. After a time, they parted ways. The church blessed them both as they laid hands on them and sent them in opposite directions.

Because of that parting of ways, two mission works were established instead of one. This event also helped young John Mark, who went with his cousin Barnabas, to mature and become a leader and author of the Gospel of Mark. Yet, I am not sure I like that process or outcome. Why can't everyone just get along and love each other? That would change the outcome. Yet, God redeems the worst situations and glorifies Himself.

There are so many suffering people sitting in the pews of our churches today. It wasn't just the two of us questioning God and being broken. Pastor Joseph Parker once said to aspiring young pastors, "Preach to the suffering and you will never lack a congregation. There is a broken heart in every pew."

"Life happens. God is not caught off guard or by surprise. It may take us a while to catch our breath, to ride the wave, to trust that God has something in mind—something good—that we would never have dreamed." (Paula Rinehart)

We are to rejoice and be glad that God permits problems because they result in upgrades of provision, promise and favor. Who doesn't want that? We see those results on this side of our pit time. In newness of life I change my thinking, perception and language and continue to practice until I *become* it. Our faith is increased by experiencing trouble. Problems come because it gives us the opportunity to exercise faith and learn to depend on God. In turn we can use our deepened faith to encourage one another because of what we have learned through it all. My story propels me toward freedom, endurance, faith, hope, and forgiveness.

God's gift of grace tracks throughout our story. Think how you and I can change the world with our stories. What if Moses said, "I don't do Red Seas"? Or Noah said, "I don't do arks"? What if Jesus said, "I don't do crosses"? My situation is never hopeless. I am never alone—He walks with me or even carries me in the hardest places. I can never lose. I am "more than a conqueror through Him who loved me and gave Himself for me."

This has been one of my favorite Bible passages in the last years: "But for me, I'm not giving up. I'm sticking around to see what God will do. I'm waiting for God to make things right. I'm counting on God to listen to me. Don't, enemy, crow over me. I'm down, but I'm not out. I'm sitting in the dark right now, but God is my light. I can take God's punishing rage, I deserve it—I sinned. But it's not forever. He's on my side and is going to get me out of this. He'll turn the lights on and show me His ways. I'll see the whole picture and how right He is. And my enemy will see it too, and be discredited—yes disgraced! This enemy who kept taunting, 'So where is this God of yours?' I'm going to see it with these, my own eyes—my enemy disgraced, trash in the gutter. Oh, that will be a day! A day for rebuilding your city; a day for stretching your arms, spreading your wings!" (Micah 7:7-11, *MSG*)

We are made new by God, in His grace, as we account to Him regarding all our disarray and messes. We are spreading our wings and flying again! You remember that wall hanging my sister gave me, "*Your beautifully messy story matters. Tell it!*" That is what I am doing here and now, to show that the power in us comes from God Himself. He enters our story—to astound us and to transform us into the new. He has rescued us into a new nature.

I now see our story in a new way. I see it as a grace and not a mess. I cannot dwell on where I've been but I need to prepare my mind for where I'm going. I've seen this attributed to several sources: "Only God can turn a mess into a message, a test into a testimony, a trial into a triumph, a problem into a prayer and a victim into a victory. Don't give up now." God can use our pain as a pulpit to inspire someone else. He's turning scars into character.

"It is probable that God lets every human being that crosses our path meet us in order that we may have the opportunity of leaving some blessing in his path and dropping into his heart and life some influence that will draw him nearer to God." (A. B. Simpson) Each and every person who crosses my path in a given day is sent by God for some purpose. I can make a difference in that life.

"Scripture says that a thousand generations can reap the benefits of God's gracious favor over one who loved Him and followed Him feverishly and obediently. God has the capacity to mark my entire family line and descendants with blessing." (Beth Moore) Bring it on! May it be so! May we learn from the journey and pass truth on to the next generations.

I do not desire that the rush of every-day urgency obscures the depth of the past. We need to review life events, remember them, renew them, rely on them and relay the truth of God's faithfulness *through* them to our children. Just like my parents and grandparents relayed them to me. How His Word provides the sure footing and truth we need even when surrounded by the muck of uncertainty in today's world!

The generations to come should know that God loves deserts because He loves to redeem people and bad situations. He loves to take broken or dead dreams and fill them with life and beauty. He loves deserts because it is the best place for Him to show His power to redeem.

My greatest test and brokenness may become my greatest ministry. What has happened only serves to make Christ more perfectly known. I desire to help others going through their own tests. Philippians 1:19: "Yes, I will continue to rejoice, for I know that through your prayers and the help given by the Spirit of Jesus Christ, what has happened to me will turn out for my deliverance. I eagerly expect and hope that I will…have sufficient courage so that now as always Christ will be exalted in my body, whether by life or by death."

God's chisel will do His transforming work. "The tool God uses the most is suffering, adversity, difficulty, hard times, irritations, struggles, and opposition. Suffering produces perseverance; perseverance, character, and character, hope. Adversity strips us down, exposes us, and breaks us—all prerequisites for genuine spiritual growth. Suffering makes us aware of our need, our weakness and our sinfulness. It drives us to God." (Jerry Sittser)

No matter what the cause of our suffering or loss we can conclude that God is Sovereign and has a larger purpose in our pain. We cannot assume that pain surprises, outwits or thwarts the plan of God or His purposes. "The Lord will fulfill His purposes for me." (Psalm 138:8) "God is completely dependable; He will not let me down." (I Peter 4:19)

Life often falls apart. We cannot live up to God's standards—we fall short and we fail. It affirms our need of redemption. There are no limits to what God can do. His character will be developed in us as we are refined like gold. If you are a child of God you will be no stranger to the rod. You must pass through the fire to come out as gold. It's His love! Restoration is the nature of God. It will come. Wait for it!

Our predicament or wounding never puts God off from loving us and walking through it with us. We celebrate the knowledge and wisdom we gained through our experiences. God is moved by our faith as we choose to redeem the past. We desire to be strengthened, lengthened, stretched, our territory enlarged in some way, because there are no boundaries with God. Opportunities exist as the Lord leads you to riches in secret places, breakthrough, turn-around, and abundance where there has been lack.

The Prayer of Jabez reminds us that God has no limits and that He cares for us. Isaiah 54:3-8 in *The Message* says it like this: "Clear lots of ground for your tents! Make your tents large. Spread out. Think big! Use plenty of rope, drive the tent pegs deep. You're going to need lots of elbow room for your growing family. You're going to take over whole nations; you're going to resettle abandoned cities. Don't be afraid—you're not going to be embarrassed. Don't hold back—you're not going to come up short…For your Maker is your bridegroom, his name, God-of-the-Angel-Armies! …I left you, but only for a moment. Now, with enormous compassion, I'm bringing you back…It's with lasting love that I'm tenderly caring for you." Ah, may it be so. Amen!

I am writing this part of my life story especially for our kids and grandkids. May all who come behind us find us faithful. Let all the generations sing of His love forever, hear and rejoice! He is good!

Dear one, what is your desperate situation today? What is in your hand that you are holding tightly? Where are you? Start there. Open and freely declare your need to the One who cares deeply for you. The God of Elijah the prophet or Joseph of the pit lives to help you. The God of angel armies! He desires that you lack no good thing. Approach Him with open hands. Approach the Lord of Hosts by speaking His name out loud. That name has power, might and His name will break every stronghold which is keeping you from becoming all He created you to be. His name is life, healing, His name gives sight and insight. His name will free every captive. That name brings light and He is life. His name is above all others. Jesus!

The God who created, redeemed and loves us will never forsake us. We are not abandoned! Our time of spiritual trial and dryness will pass, just as winter passes into spring, just as drought eventually is relieved by rainfall. We will be frustrated if we depend on the rain. If we sink our roots into the subsoil of God's love, if we look not to our dire circumstances but to the certainty of God's faithfulness, we can endure anything.

The good news is that we will discover Divine refuge when we realize the fact that sometimes seasons are hard and dry and that God is in charge of both. Then the hope is not in us but in God. He shelters us under His wings until the season improves and we can again bear fruit.

Ravi Zacharias says that if there is an author of life, then there is a script and a story. God is *in* my story. "God is not only the author in *description*, but He is also the author in *prescription*. Not only is God holy, but He reveals to us the sacred nature of love, to which He beckons us. And from this sacredness of His love must flow all other loves." My response is love and worship.

I celebrate a new time of opportunity and change, the redemption of the past that brought failure or sorrow. I celebrate what I learned and gleaned from walking in His Spirit in every circumstance.

"May God, who puts all things together, makes all things whole, Who made a lasting mark through the sacrifice of Jesus, Who led Jesus, our Great Shepherd, up and alive from the dead, Now put you together, provide you with everything you need to please him, Make us into what gives him most pleasure, by means of the sacrifice of Jesus, the Messiah. All glory to Jesus forever and always! Oh, yes, yes, yes." (Hebrews 13:20-21, *MSG*)

My story is not over; it is still being written. Every day of my life is in His Sovereign will and care. Every day we can choose what we do with each moment and how we will respond to it. I am continually working on a life of gratitude and forgiveness. It is a process. A growing sense of inner peace flows as I remember that God's chapters are still being written. This isn't *the end.* "Because of the Lord's great love we are not consumed, for his compassions never fail. They are new every morning; great is His faithfulness." (Lamentations 3:22-23) And through it all I know He has the last word! The very last word! "I'm on my way! I'll be there soon! Yes! Come Master Jesus!" (Revelation 22:20, *MSG*)

Praise the name of the Lord! God is good and faithful to all generations! Hear and rejoice!

CHAPTER 31

Bene Dictus (Good Saying)

THE FOLLOWING SCRIPTURES and quotes are random, from my journal. These good sayings include the abridged consequences, reasons, and steps toward forgiveness:

Consequences of an unforgiving spirit: (R. T. Kendall, selected from *Total Healing*)

1 The Holy Spirit is grieved. (Matthew 6:15; Ephesians 4:30) I am left to myself. (Proverbs 14:14) God doesn't help anyone moving in his own strength. Sin gives free reign for Satan to come in and take advantage of me. In that, I am doing GOD'S job.
2 I force God to become my enemy. (James 4:1-4)
3 I lose the potential of my anointing. (Romans 11:29)
4 I have no authentic fellowship with the Father; I become an empty shell. (Matthew 7:1, 2; Luke 6:37) Do not judge, or you too will be judged, and the measure you use will be measured to you. We "play God" when we judge people or unfairly criticize them.

Reasons to forgive: (R. T. Kendall, selected from *Total Healing*)

1 Consider the consequences if you do not forgive.
2 Release those who have wronged you and you will be released. Releasing the bondage of unforgiveness will bring peace.
3 God may use you down the road if you set your enemies free and never look back. (Matthew 6:15)

Steps in total forgiveness of others: (R. T. Kendall, selected from *Total Healing*)

1. Make a deliberate and irrevocable choice not to tell anyone what they did. Keep quiet.
2. Be pleasant to them should you be around them; put them at ease.
3. If conversation ensues, say that which would set them free from guilt, like Joseph to his brothers. (Genesis 45:5; Luke 6:31)
4. Let them feel good about themselves.
5. Protect them from their greatest fear (that secrets won't be revealed).
6. Keep it up today, tomorrow, this year and next.
7. Pray for them that they would be blessed and prosper.

What total forgiveness is: (R. T. Kendall, selected from *Total Healing*)

1. Being aware of what someone has done and still forgiving them.
2. Choosing to keep no record of wrongs. (I Corinthians 13:5) This is not a feeling, but an act of the will.
3. Refusing to punish. Don't seek revenge. (I John 4:18) Wanting your enemies punished will eventually lead to a loss of the anointing of the Spirit.
4. Not telling what they did.
5. Being merciful. (Matthew 5:7) As God is just and merciful carrying our punishment, so this belongs to God alone. (Luke 6:36)
6. Graciousness shown. Overlooking what you perceive to be truth and not letting on about anything that could be damaging to the other person.
7. It is an inner heart condition. Matthew 12:34 says out of the overflow of the heart the mouth speaks.
8. It is the absence of bitterness and resentment and vengeance. This negates irritability, control, insomnia, high blood pressure, depression, isolation, a constant negative perspective. As you

have gentleness of spirit you relinquish bitterness and the Holy Spirit is free to move in with His peace, joy and knowledge of His will.

9 Forgiving God. Bitterness is traced to resentment of God for allowing evil and suffering.

10 Forgiving ourselves. Be filled with joy. In forgiving ourselves we can forgive others and as in Joseph's story God will promote us in His time.

Ten steps to freedom -- good to keep in mind as I move forward: (edit from R. T. Kendall, *Total Healing*)

1 Stop excusing, rationalizing, defending.
2 Pinpoint actions that have hurt me.
3 Life is more satisfying if you let go of grievances.
4 Replace angry thoughts about those who hurt me with thoughts about how they are also vulnerable human beings.
5 Identify with others' probable state of mind (knowing history). Understand their motives.
6 Develop a greater compassion toward them.
7 Become more aware of my own need of forgiveness in the past.
8 Resolve to not pass on my own pain to others.
9 Then appreciate a sense of purpose and direction.
10 Enjoy the sense of emotional relief that comes when the burden of a grudge has gone away. Enjoy feelings of goodwill and mercy I can and will show.

"Imagine yourself as a living house. God comes in to rebuild that house. At first, perhaps, you can understand what He is doing. He is getting the drains right and stopping the leaks in the roof and so on; you knew that those jobs needed doing and so you are not surprised. But presently He starts knocking the house about in a way that hurts abominably and does not seem to make any sense. What on earth is He up to?

The explanation is that He is building quite a different house from the one you thought of—throwing out a new wing here, putting on an extra floor there, running up towers, making courtyards. You thought you were being made into a decent little cottage: but He is building a palace. He intends to come and live in it Himself." (C. S. Lewis)

"God begins His greatest work when the inner man is opened to Him. God will wound you deeply. For in this way, He continues to open all the inner chambers of your soul. Such disturbance marks your best chance of hearing his voice in the deep places where your heart makes up its mind. In all this wounding, God is opening the way to the central chamber of your soul. There He plans to set before you a feast. This is the banquet place of the Holy Spirit...Pain is often the megaphone that awakens." (Saint John of the Cross, writing more than 400 years ago about the mysterious and unexpected way in which God draws our hearts to his).

"How much evidence of God's faithfulness will it take before we learn to trust Him? Refusing to believe God, even though He continues to provide for us, is an affront to our loving God." Numbers 14:11: "The Lord said to Moses, how long will these people reject me? And how long will they not believe me, with all the signs which I have performed among them?" (Henry and Richard Blackaby from *Waiting on God: Trust in His Timing*)

Isaiah 49:16-18, *MSG*: "I'd never forget you—never. Look, I've written your names on the backs of my hands. The walls you're rebuilding are never out of my sight. Your builders are faster than your wreckers. The demolition crews are gone for good. Look up, look around, look well! See them all gathering, coming to you? As sure as I am the living God—God's Decree—you're going to put them on like so much jewelry, you're going to use them to dress up like a bride."

"The roots grow deep when the winds are strong." (Chuck Swindoll)

"Pain insists upon being attended to. God whispers to us in our pleasures, speaks in our consciences, but shouts in our pains. It is his megaphone to rouse a deaf world." (C.S. Lewis)

"Difficulty is inevitable. Drama is a choice." (Anita Renfroe)

"I have held many things in my hands," Martin Luther once said, "and I have lost them all; but whatever I have placed in God's hands, that, I still possess." Jerry Sittser says to "pray with open hands, a posture that symbolizes your desire to surrender your will to God. Don't try to change your circumstances when you pray—God uses our circumstances to change us. Surrender yourself to God."

"We should pray for deliverance from our selfish interests, not for their fulfillment." (John Cassian)

"Praying means giving up a false security, no longer looking for arguments which will protect you if you get pushed into a corner, no longer setting your hope on a couple of lighter moments which your life might still offer. To pray means to stop expecting from God the small mindedness which you discover in yourself." (Henri Nouwen)

"When we pray we decide to leave an ego-centered world and enter a God-centered world. This is not easy. We are used to anxieties, egos, problems—we are not used to wonder, God and mystery." (Eugene Peterson)

"Pray for our heart's desire, but with flexibility as well as boldness, holding our expectations with a light touch and looking for signs that God is answering our prayers differently than we wanted or asked for. Unanswered prayer from our limited perspective might in fact turn out to be answered prayer from a larger frame of reference—the bigger picture." (Jerry Sittser)

"If there is any way God can surpass our requests, He will; Ole Hallesby acknowleged that such an answer to prayer might appear to us to be unanswered prayer. Using Luther as an example, Hallesby wrote, 'As Luther says, we pray for silver, but God often gives us gold instead.' Every time Jesus sees that there is a possibility of giving us more than we know how to ask, He does so. And in order to do so He often has to deal with us in ways which are past our finding out." (Ole Hallesby taken from *When God Doesn't Answer Your Prayer* by Jerry Sittser)

"Anything big enough to occupy our minds is big enough to hang a prayer on." (George MacDonald)

"This is a fallen world and some part of that ruin has invaded my life... The whole notion that some part of the pain of life is unavoidable is not an easy idea to confront, especially for Christians. We tend to see our lives as a series of hurdles, which, if we trust God and jump high enough, we can get through without scraping our knees. If we miss a hurdle, though—or come through bloody and bruised—we must have done it wrong. We have failed. Or worse, God has failed us." (Paula Rinehart)

Job 42:2-6 speaks of Job becoming utterly still and silent, struck dumb by the unspeakable presence of God. He had no more questions, he made no more demands, he claimed no more rights. He simply bowed and surrendered and got what he needed the most: an encounter with the living God.

"The scandal of God's silence in the most heartbreaking hours of our journey is perceived in retrospect as veiled tender Presence and a passage into pure trust that is not at the mercy of the response it receives." (Brennan Manning) "What seems like God's silence can be the gateway into a trust that is not dependent on circumstances—one that trusts on the basis deeper than what is seen." (Paula Rinehart)

"We're building up or tearing down in all we do. Are we on the construction gang or on the wrecking crew? He has the right to criticize who has the heart to help." (Abraham Lincoln)

"While the trial lasts the strength is equal to the emergency; but when it is over, natural weakness claims the right to show itself...Before any great achievement some measure of the same depression is very usual." (Charles Spurgeon)

"God is for you. Turn to the sidelines; that's God cheering your run. Look past the finish line; that's God applauding your steps." (Max Lucado)

"Worrying is carrying tomorrow's load with today's strength – carrying two days at once. It is moving into tomorrow ahead of time. Worrying doesn't empty tomorrow of its sorrow, it empties today of its strength... Worry is a cycle of inefficient thoughts whirling around a center of fear." (Corrie ten Boom)

"Jesus knows how you feel. You are precious to Him. So precious that He became like you so that you would come to Him. When you struggle, He listens. When you yearn, He responds. When you question, He hears." (Max Lucado)

Psalm 34:4, 6… "from my fears…out of all his troubles"… My fear is not (the same as) yours, but nearly everyone has, somewhere inside, a weary little fear which keeps cropping up. But every time the fear pushes out its head, there, waiting to end it is that glorious word "delivered from all my fears" (not from some, or from most, but from *all*). "Out of all his troubles." This may find someone in trouble. We may have to pass through the waters, but we shall be delivered out of them. They will not overflow us. When the man cried and the Lord heard him, he was saved out of *all* his troubles." (Excerpts from Amy Carmichael's *Edges of His Ways*)

Faith is:

- something God will prove genuine, by testing
- developed through hardship, disappointment, conflict, disillusionment, frustration, failure, loss
- refusal to worry even when I haven't a clue as to what God would have me to do next
- thanking God when I am left with shattered plans and dreams that He has better plans
- claiming God's strength to patiently accept and endure weariness, pain, rejection, betrayal and abandonment, woundedness and decline
- expecting a sea of golden grain from the bleak, barren, endless fields, watered only by my tears
- the assurance that God is perfecting His design for me when my life's course, once a swift-flowing current, seems a stagnant pool
- standing on the fact that God has designed me flawlessly for His purpose in the universe when I feel like everything about me is one big mistake

- recognizing that God is the Lord of time when my idea of timing doesn't agree with His
- confidence in God when money is running out and not rolling in
- allowing God to straighten the record when false things have been said about me
- remembering I am indispensable to God when I feel I only clutter up the landscape
- knowing that God will turn my grievous circumstances around for His ultimate good
- ceasing to worry, leaving the future to the God who controls the future
- stepping out onto the water when we don't understand what can possibly hold us up
- rounding the bend into a branch of the river we have never traveled
- the assurance and hope that although the future may be unknown to us, it is not in the least unfamiliar to the One who leads us (Excerpts from *Faith Is* by Pamela Reeve, Multnomah Press)

Proverbs 3:21-26, *MSG*: "Dear friend, guard Clear Thinking and Common Sense with your life; don't for a minute lose sight of them. They'll keep your soul alive and well, they'll keep you fit and attractive. You'll travel safely, you'll neither tire nor trip. You'll take afternoon naps without a worry, you'll enjoy a good night's sleep. No need to panic over alarms or surprises, or predictions that doomsday's just around the corner, Because God will be right there with you; He'll keep you safe and sound."

God is always thinking about us. His thoughts toward me are tender and loving. Knowing this allows me to persevere. Not a pang of sorrow escapes Him. In our labor He marks our weariness and writes in His book all our struggles.

My friend Linda Koblish told me on April 22, 2004, "The unknowns are only unknown to us and not to the Lord." As Corrie ten Boom said, "Never be afraid to trust an unknown future to a known God."

"Guard my life and rescue me, O Lord. Let me not be put to shame, for I take refuge in you. May integrity and uprightness protect me, because my hope is in you." (Psalm 25:20, 21) Psalm 35:22-24: "O Lord, you have seen this; be not silent. Do not be far from me, O Lord. Awake, and rise to my defense! Contend for me, my God and my Lord. Vindicate me in your righteousness, O Lord my God. Do not let them gloat over me." (From my sister on February 14, 2004)

"All we have to decide is what to do with the time given us." (J. R. R. Tolkien)

"Just because the past didn't turn out like you wanted it to, doesn't mean your future can't be better than you ever imagined." (Unknown)

I Peter 5:5-7, *MSG*: "God has had it with the proud, but takes delight in just plain people. So be content with who you are, and don't put on airs. God's strong hand is on you. He'll promote you at the right time. Live carefree (free of anxiety) before God; He is most careful with you."

"The deepest level of worship is praising God in spite of the pain, thanking God during the trials, trusting Him when we're tempted to lose hope and loving Him when he seems so distant and far away. At my lowest, God is my hope. At my darkest, God is my light. At my weakest, God is my strength. At my saddest, God is my comforter." (Spiritual inspiration from *Touching Lives* on Facebook)

"Don't embarrass me by not showing up." (Psalm 31:15) Has anything in your fields—vine, fig tree, pomegranate, olive tree—failed to flourish? "From now on you can count on a blessing." (Haggai 2: 19b)

"God has left some useful thorns and thistles in my garden to keep me from making myself at home in the fertilizer." (Beth Moore) We grow in the valley because that's where all the fertilizer is! Learn to welcome the valley times and see all the growth in character that comes from them. And know that God always provides in an isolation time.

Isaiah 41:17-20: "The poor and needy search for water, but there is none; their tongues are parched with thirst. But I the Lord will answer them; I, the God of Israel, will not forsake them. I will make rivers flow on barren heights, and springs within the valleys. I will turn the desert into pools of water, and the parched ground into springs. I will put in the desert the cedar and the acacia, the myrtle and the olive. I will set pines in the wasteland, the fir and the cypress together, so that people may see and know, may consider and understand that the hand of the Lord has done this, that the Holy One of Israel has created it."

"You can never learn that Christ is all you need, until Christ is all you have." (Corrie ten Boom)

"There is no pit so deep that God's love is not deeper still." (Corrie ten Boom)

Jeremiah 17:7-8 "But blessed is the man who trusts in the Lord, whose confidence is in Him. He will be like a tree planted by the water that sends out its roots by the stream. It does not fear when heat comes; its leaves are always green. It has no worries in a year of drought and never fails to bear fruit."

In reviewing Job's life: "Calamity is not proof of guilt." (Charles Swindoll)

"To live with the Sacred is hard. It means that we walk with a God who does not explain himself to us. It means that we worship a God who is mysterious—too mysterious to fit our formulas for better living. It means that God is not our best friend, our secret lover or our alter ego. It even means that it is just as frightening as it is delightful to stand in His presence. Our creaturely relationship with God is one in which we are, at the same time, both irresistibly drawn to Him and humbled by the grandeur of His holiness." (M. Craig Barnes, *Yearning*)

"God wants to change *us* to His liking—not change the *world* to our liking." (Eugene Peterson)

The sunshine still shines even though the clouds obscure the mountains. So God's providence cannot obscure our faith through difficulties. Our sorrows, losses and adversities are preparation for knowing God more. (Unknown)

Habakkuk 3:17-19, *MSG*: "Though the cherry trees don't blossom and the strawberries don't ripen, Though the apples are worm-eaten and the wheat fields are stunted, Though the sheep pens are sheepless and the cattle barns empty, I'm singing joyful praise to God. I'm turning cartwheels of joy to my Savior God. Counting on God's Rule to prevail, I take heart and gain strength. I run like a deer. I feel like I'm king of the mountain! (For congregational use, with a full orchestra)."

Nahum 1:7, *MSG*: "God is good, a hiding place in tough times. He recognizes and welcomes anyone looking for help, no matter how desperate the trouble. But cozy islands of escape He wipes right off the map."

Isaiah 61:1-4 declares the year of the Lord's favor: "The Spirit of the Sovereign Lord is on me because the Lord is on me, because the Lord has anointed me to preach good news to the poor. He sent me to bind up the brokenhearted, to proclaim freedom for the captives, and release from darkness for the prisoners, to proclaim the year of the Lord's favor... to comfort all who mourn and provide for those who grieve, to bestow on them a crown of beauty instead of ashes, strength instead of fear, the oil of gladness instead of mourning, and a garment of praise instead of a spirit of despair. They will be called oaks of righteousness, a planting of the Lord for the display of His splendor. They will rebuild the ruins and restore the places long devastated."

"God uses people who fail because there aren't any other kind around." (John C. Maxwell)

"Don't assume a conspiracy when incompetence explains it all." (John Goodwin)

I've been encouraged by the message of Mrs. Beaver in C. S. Lewis' *The Lion, Witch and Wardrobe*. Mr. and Mrs. Beaver are describing to Lucy and Peter the one who can rescue Narnia from evil and danger—a lion named Aslan who is the Christ figure. Lucy is not so sure that she's ready to meet such a dangerous creature. "Then is He safe, Mrs. Beaver," asked Lucy? "Safe?" asked Mrs. Beaver. "Who said anything about safe? Course He isn't safe. But He's good."

"Even the storms bear a message of encouragement for us: Deeper roots make for stronger lives." From Ephesians 3:17, 18: "And I pray that you, being rooted and established in love, may have power to grasp how wide and long and high and deep is the love of Christ." (Charles R. Swindoll, *The Grace of Encouragement*)

"We are not necessarily doubting that God will do the best for us; we are wondering how painful the best will turn out to be." (C.S. Lewis)

II Corinthians 4:8-10: "We are pressed on every side by troubles, but we are not crushed or broken. We are perplexed, but not driven to despair. (We don't give up and quit). We are hunted down, but *never abandoned* by God. We get knocked down, but we are not destroyed (we get up again and keep going). Through suffering, these bodies of ours constantly share in the death of Jesus so that the life of Jesus may also be seen in our bodies." (Parentheses are mine)

"Appreciate your pastoral leaders who gave you the Word of God. Take a good look at the way they live, and let their faithfulness instruct you. There should be a consistency that runs through us all. For Jesus doesn't change—yesterday, today, tomorrow, he's always totally himself." (Hebrews 13:7, 8, *MSG*)

"As long as you have a pulse, God has a plan." (Unknown)

I release the past to you, God. I open my hands. Thank you for the peace it brings! Root out the hidden and hardened places if resentment remains. You forgive totally and you expect no less from me! Amen!

The godly hero, in order to be useful as an instrument of significance in the Lord's hand, must be humbled and forced to trust.

"Consecrate yourselves for tomorrow you (God) will do amazing things among us." (Joshua 3:5)

This is all for God's glory! The story is still being written. Let the generations hear and rejoice! God is good! Amen!

Resource Bibliography

Allender, Dan. *Leading With a Limp.* WaterBrook Press.

Allender, Dr. Dan, and Longman III, Dr. Tremper. *Cry of the Soul.* Nav Press.

Arterburn, Stephen. *Healing Is A Choice.* Thomas Nelson.

Arthur, Kay. *Lord Where Are You When Bad Things Happen?* WaterBrook Press.

Barnes, Emilie. *A Different Kind of Miracle (Hope, Healing and God's Faithfulness).* Harvest House.

Biebel, David. *If God is So Good, Why Do I Hurt So Bad*? Revell.

Blackaby, Henry and Richard. *Waiting on God: Trust in His Timing.* Thomas Nelson.

Buckingham, Jamie. *A Way Through the Wilderness.* Chosen Books.

Buechner, Frederick. *Whistling in the Dark.* HarperOne.

Burchett, Dave. *Bring 'Em Back Alive.* WaterBrook Press.

Carson, D.A. *How Long, O Lord? Reflections on Suffering and Evil.* Baker Book House.

Christianson, Evelyn. *Gaining Through Losing: How Hurts and Tragedies Can be Turned into Spiritual Gains.* Chariot Victor Publishing.

Clairmont, Patsy. *Mending Your Heart in a Broken World.* Warner Books.

Cloud, Dr. Henry and Townsend, Dr. John. *What to Do When You Don't Know What to Do: God Will Make a Way).* Integrity Publishing.

Cloud, Dr. Henry. *Changes That Heal (When Your World Makes No Sense).* Zondervan.

Crabb, Larry. *Shattered Dreams: God's Unexpected Path to Joy.* Water Brook Press.

Cymbala, Jim. *Storm: Hearing Jesus for the Times We Live In.* Zondervan

DeMoss, Nancy Leigh. *Choosing Forgiveness: Your Journey to Freedom.* Moody Publishers.

Dillow, Linda. *Calm My Anxious Heart.* Nav Press Publishing Group.

Dillow, Linda. *Steadfast Faith in the Midst of Adversity.* Nav Press Publishing Group.

Edwards, Gene. *A Study in Brokenness.* Christian Books.

Edwards, Gene. *Exquisite Agony: Crucified by Christians.* SeedSowers.

Edwards, Gene. *Prisoner In the Third Cell.* Tyndale House.

Eldredge, John and Stasi. *Captivating.* Thomas Nelson.

Elliot, Elisabeth. *A Slow and Certain Light (Guidance).* Fleming H Revell Company.

Elliot, Elisabeth. *Keep a Quiet Heart.* Vine Books.

Elliot, Elisabeth. *Trusting God in a Twisted World (On Asking God Why).* Fleming H Revell.

Ellis, Gwen. *A Quiet Place: Discovering the Pleasure of Prayer.* Zondervan.

Evans, David G. and Horner, Danielle. *Healed Without Scars (Path to Wholeness in Christ).* Whitaker House.

Gire, Ken. *Windows of the Soul (Experiencing God in New Ways).* Zondervan.

Greenfield, Guy. *The Wounded Minister (Healing From Personal Attack).* Baker, 2001.

Guthrie, Nancy. *Holding on to Hope: A Pathway through Suffering to the Heart of God.* Tindale.

Hammond, Michelle McKinney. *Wounded Hearts, Renewed Hope: Meditations for Those on the Healing Path.* Harvest House Publishers.

Hartman, Jack. *Never, Never Give Up.* Lamplight Ministries Publication.

Hearn, Marie Malcom. *Demolishing Strongholds (To Walk in Freedom).* Self published.

Jensen, Margaret. *A Nail in a Sure Place (Holding On When you Want to Let Go).* Harvest Publishing.

Jeremiah, David. *When Your World Falls Apart: Seeing Past the Pain of the Present.* Turning Point.

Johnson, Barbara. *Valley of Despair.* Inspirational Press.

Keller, Timothy. *Walking With God Through Pain and Suffering.* Dutton.

Kendall, R. T. *Total Forgiveness.* Charisma House.

Kent, Carol. *A New Kind of Normal: Hope-Filled Choices When Life Turns Upside Down*. Thomas Nelson.

Kent, Carol. *When I Lay My Isaac Down: Unshakable Faith in Unthinkable Circumstances*. Nav Press.

LaHaye, Beverly. *A Different Kind of Strength*. Harvest House, 2001.

Lewis, C.S. *The Problem of Pain*. Macmillan Publishing Company.

Lotz, Anne Graham. *Wounded by God's People. Why?* Zondervan.

Lucado, Max. *Grace For the Moment*. Thomas Nelson.

Lucado, Max. *You'll Get Through This: Hope and Help for your Turbulent Times*. Thomas Nelson.

Lyda, Hope. *One Minute Prayers For Those Who Hurt*. Harvest House Publishers.

Mansfield, Stephen. *Healing Your Church Hurt*. Tindale Momentum.

Merton, Thomas. *The Wisdom of the Desert*. New Directions Publishing Corporation.

Manuel, Esther. *Treasures of Darkness: Finding Hope Stronger Than Our Hurts*. Essence Publishing.

Maynard, Dennis R. *When Sheep Attack!* Dennis R. Maynard, self-published.

Metzgar Margaret. *A Time to Mourn, A Time to Dance: Help for the Losses in Life*. Thrivent Lutheran.

Meyer, F.B. *The Gift of Suffering.* Kregel Publishing.

Moore, Beth. *Praying God's Word: Breaking Free From Spiritual Strongholds.* Broadman and Holman.

Moore, Beth. *Get Out of That Pit.* Integrity Publishers, division of Thomas Nelson.

Nouwen, Henri J.M. *Wounded Healer.* Image Books.

Omartian, Stormie. *A Story of Forgiveness and Healing.* Harvest House.

Omartian, Stormie. *Just Enough Light for the Step I'm On: Trusting God in Tough Times.* Harvest House.

Peterson, Eugene. *The Message/Remix.* Nav Press.

Piper, John. *The Roots of Endurance (Perseverance).* Crossway Books.

Rikkers, Doris, Compiler. *Hope For A Woman's Soul.* Inspirio, Zondervan.

Schmidt, Frederick W., Jr. *When Suffering Persists.* Moorehouse Publishing, 2001.

Schuller, Robert. *Life's Not Fair, But God is Good.* Thomas Nelson.

Seamands, David. *Healing For Damaged Emotions.* David C Cook.

Shepson, Charles. *From My Grieving Heart to Yours.* Toccoa Falls Press, 1996.

Sittser, Jerry. *A Grace Disguised: How the Soul Grows Through Loss.* Zondervan.

Sittser, Jerry. *The Will of God As a Way of Life*. Zondervan.

Sittser, Jerry. *When God Doesn't Answer Your Prayer*. Zondervan.

Smedes, Lewis. *Forgive and Forget*. Pocket Publishing, 1984.

Smith, Gwen. *Broken Into Beautiful: How God Restores the Wounded Heart*. Harvest House Publishers.

Sorge, Bob. *Pain, Perplexity, and Promotion (on Book and Life of Job)*. Oasis House.

Sorge, Bob. *The Fire of Delayed Answers*. Oasis House.

Southerland, Mary. *Sandpaper People: Dealing With Ones Who Rub You the Wrong Way*. Harvest House.

Stiller, Brian J. *When Life Hurts (Path to Healing)*. Herald Press.

Stokes, Penelope J. *Beside a Quiet Stream (Words of Hope for Weary Hearts)*. Thomas Nelson.

Susek, Ron. *Firestorm*. Baker Books, 1999.

Swenson, Dr. Richard. *The Overload Syndrome*. Nav Press.

Swindoll, Charles. *Come Before Winter*. Living Books.

Swindoll, Charles. *Avoiding Stress Fractures*. Zondervan.

Swindoll, Charles. *Elijah: A Man of Heroism and Humility*. Word Publishing.

Swindoll, Charles. *Hope Again (When Life Hurts and Dreams Fade).* Word Publishing.

Swindoll, Charles. *Perfect Trust.* J Countryman Publishers.

Swindoll, Charles. *Recovery: When Healing Takes Time* (physical healing). Word Books.

Swindoll, Charles. *Second Wind: Fresh Hope for the Road Ahead.* Zondervan.

Swindoll, Charles. *Three Steps Forward, Two Steps Back: Persevering Through Pressure.* Bantam Books.

Tada, Joni Eareckson. *A Place of Healing.* David C. Cook.

Trebesch, Shelley. *Isolation (A Place of Transformation in the Life of a Leader).* Barnabas Publishers.

Van Vonderen, Jeff. *When God's People Let You Down.* Bethany House Publishers.

Voskamp, Ann. *One Thousand Gifts.* Zondervan.

Walsh, Sheila. *God Loves Broken People: And Those Who Pretend They're Not.* Thomas Nelson.

Walsh, Sheila. *Life is Tough But God is Faithful: How to See God's Love in Difficult Times.* Thomas Nelson.

Wolfelt, Alan D., Dr. *Understanding Your Grief: Ten Essential Touchstones for Finding Hope and Healing In Your Heart.* Companion Press.

Wright, H. Norman. *Recovering from Losses in Life.* Revell.

Yancey, Philip. *Disappointment With God.* Zondervan.

Yancey, Philip. *Where is God When It Hurts.* Zondervan, 1997.

Zacharias, Ravi and Vitale, Vince. *Why Suffering?* FaithWords Publishing.

Zacharias, Ravi. *Cries of the Heart: Bringing God Near When He Feels Far Away.* Word

Zempel, Heather. *Amazed and Confused: When God's Actions Collide With Our Expectations.* Thomas Nelson

35566883R00130

Made in the USA
San Bernardino, CA
28 June 2016